LIVING RIVER

DAVE SHOWALTER

Foreword by Anne Castle

LIVING RIVER

THE PROMISE OF THE MIGHTY COLORADO

BRAIDED RIVER

CONTENTS

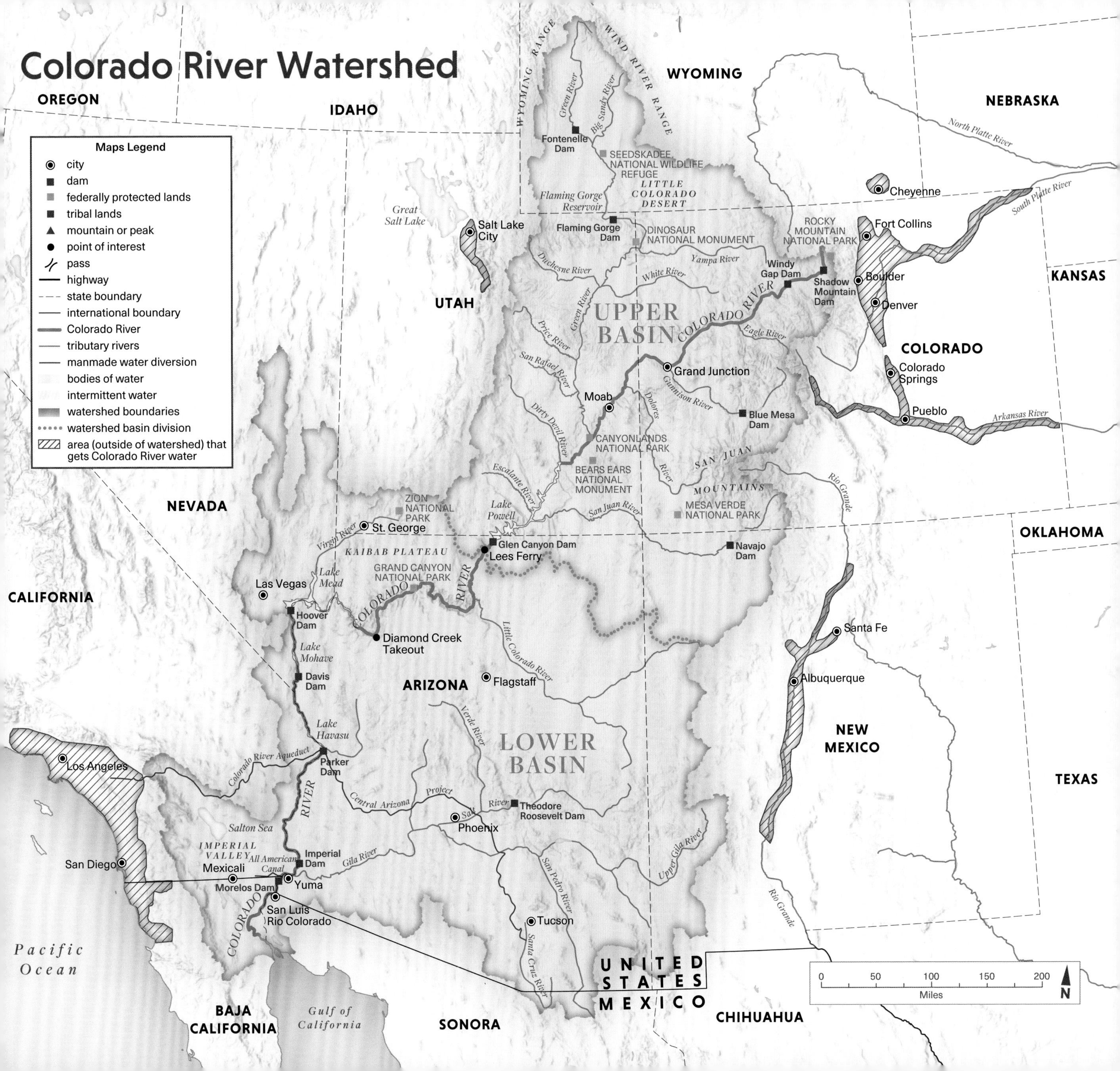
Colorado River Watershed
Maps Legend
city
dam
federally protected lands
tribal lands
mountain or peak
point of interest
pass
highway
state boundary
international boundary
Colorado River
tributary rivers
manmade water diversion
bodies of water
intermittent water
watershed boundaries
watershed basin division
area (outside of watershed) that gets Colorado River water
OREGON
IDAHO
WYOMING
NEBRASKA
UTAH
NEVADA
CALIFORNIA
ARIZONA
COLORADO
KANSAS
OKLAHOMA
NEW MEXICO
TEXAS
BAJA CALIFORNIA
SONORA
CHIHUAHUA
UNITED STATES
MEXICO
WYOMING RANGE
WIND RIVER RANGE
Green River
Big Sandy River
Fontenelle Dam
SEEDSKADEE NATIONAL WILDLIFE REFUGE
LITTLE COLORADO DESERT
Flaming Gorge Reservoir
Flaming Gorge Dam
DINOSAUR NATIONAL MONUMENT
Great Salt Lake
Salt Lake City
North Platte River
Cheyenne
South Platte River
ROCKY MOUNTAIN NATIONAL PARK
Fort Collins
Boulder
Denver
Windy Gap Dam
Shadow Mountain Dam
Yampa River
White River
Duchesne River
Green River
Price River
San Rafael River
UPPER BASIN
COLORADO RIVER
Eagle River
Grand Junction
Colorado Springs
Pueblo
Arkansas River
Moab
Gunnison River
Dolores River
Blue Mesa Dam
Dirty Devil River
CANYONLANDS NATIONAL PARK
BEARS EARS NATIONAL MONUMENT
SAN JUAN MOUNTAINS
Rio Grande
Escalante River
Lake Powell
San Juan River
MESA VERDE NATIONAL PARK
ZION NATIONAL PARK
St. George
Virgin River
KAIBAB PLATEAU
Glen Canyon Dam
Lees Ferry
Navajo Dam
Las Vegas
Lake Mead
GRAND CANYON NATIONAL PARK
COLORADO RIVER
Hoover Dam
Diamond Creek Takeout
Little Colorado River
Santa Fe
Albuquerque
Lake Mohave
Davis Dam
Flagstaff
Verde River
Lake Havasu
LOWER BASIN
Los Angeles
Colorado River Aqueduct
Parker Dam
RIVER
Central Arizona Project
Salt River
Theodore Roosevelt Dam
Phoenix
Salton Sea
IMPERIAL VALLEY
All American Canal
Imperial Dam
Gila River
Upper Gila River
San Diego
Mexicali
Morelos Dam
Yuma
San Luis Rio Colorado
COLORADO
San Pedro River
Tucson
Santa Cruz River
Rio Grande
Pacific Ocean
Gulf of California
0
50
100
150
200
Miles
N

32
34

FOREWORD

BY ANNE CASTLE

All ages are welcome at the Bears Ears Summer Gathering running race in Bears Ears National Monument, Utah.

THE COLORADO RIVER is a waterway of superlatives—the most volatile supplies, the most iconic landscapes, the most dammed, the most litigated, and, lamentably, the most threatened. It is also a river of contrasts, encompassing thriving cities juxtaposed with large swaths of rural areas where many households lack clean drinking water, whitewater rapids providing challenge and recreation upstream of a dried-up estuary, and lush and lucrative farmland whose very viability is threatened by diminished supplies.

This river is also unique in its ability to engender lifetime-long love and devotion both from residents and from distant observers. Being in some way a part of the Colorado River Basin is a source of pride, whether it stems from a deep-seated sense of belonging to the landscape, a career in the science or management of the river, or the uncomplicated enjoyment of calling this part of the nation home.

One hundred years ago, our country faced a crisis of policy—an urgent need to provide for equitable sharing of the valuable waters of the Colorado River in a manner that recognized not only existing reliance but also, more importantly, the huge future potential of the entire southwestern United States. The issue was one of defining legal rights, not limiting then-existing uses. The framers of the 1922 Colorado River Compact did the best they could, providing a foundation that has allowed the Colorado River Basin to grow from less than five hundred thousand people at the time to more than forty million today. Despite contemporary and justified criticism, the Compact must be viewed as having accomplished at least one of its purposes: securing expeditious agricultural and industrial development.

Today we face a crisis of physical forces. The river quite simply cannot provide the amount of water that residents of the basin are using. This is not a matter of minor adjustments in amounts used by some—it appears that up to one-third of the volume of existing use must be discontinued. Adjusting to that new reality, and doing so quite rapidly to prevent a catastrophic crash of the system's reservoirs, is a monumental undertaking, one that will continue through the third decade of the twenty-first century.

The Colorado River Basin is undergoing a rethinking of what we ask from the river. Learning how to live within our diminished hydrological means and how to share the burden of reduced water usage in an equitable way is difficult beyond imagining. Yet that is the task in front of us. Agreements negotiated and executed in good faith decades ago may now no longer provide the intended balance of fairness. Livelihoods are threatened, as is the unspoken assumption of many in the river community that everything must be fine so long as water continues to come out of the tap.

This midlife river crisis provides the prospect of incorporating new science, contemporary values, and long-standing unmet obligations into river management and thereby make it better. It is widely understood that the water rights, claims, and values of Native American Tribes were ignored in 1922. Moreover, no thought was given then to the value of the river as a river—it was treated as a delivery system, a network of watery input and output, and a spinner of turbines. The opportunity exists now to acknowledge the living river, with intrinsic worth in its own right as well as in its provision of the essence of life.

Challenges in the past have been overcome with achievements that matched the scope of the difficulties—significant and much-emulated breakthroughs in engineering and deal-making. The challenges of the present and future require an even greater degree of creativity and ability to see through immediate gains and losses to the greater and longer-term benefits to river interests and communities. The leaders in Colorado River water issues have historically risen to the moment, tackling tough issues when they arise, and the leadership engaged today is in the complicated and painful throes of doing so again.

The best and brightest minds in the basin are focused on solving this problem, but broader support and understanding are needed to empower water leaders to effectuate a rethinking of river relationships and uses. Recognition of the grim struggle taking place in the basin, and the alarming potential for winners and losers, is not widespread. Presentations and papers abound but cater to those already in the know. What is needed is not more experts, but a greater share of the basin's inhabitants invested in ensuring that the river ecosystem and the human community that relies on it are both sustained.

This book awakens our appreciation of the beauty and grandeur of the Colorado River, from headwaters to delta, from wild to tamed. We learn that the river represents the veins of Mother Earth, providing nutrients needed by the vegetation and fish and animal life that are fed from her body. Glimpses of the trumpeter swans, otters, and other denizens of the wintry reaches of Seedskadee National Wildlife Refuge inaugurate the journey that continues all the way to the delta, the former "milk and honey wilderness" now cracked and desiccated but with pockets of hope in the form of restored native floodplain made possible by painstaking manual labor. Aerial photography reveals the river as a fragile ribbon somehow knotting together millions of people and acres of land.

Imagery provides a visceral understanding of the value of this river. It deepens our sense of community and stimulates appreciation for the many ways in which this river is loved—and being loved to death. These stunning pictures and the stories that accompany them offer touchstones of understanding of the river's dilemma and furnish a foundation for a stronger commitment to sustainability.

Zion National Park's vertical Colorado Plateau landscape, carved by the Virgin River, is revealed from high on the Angels Landing trail. The Virgin River, the only water source for the burgeoning city of Saint George, Utah, originates north of Zion and flows 162 miles to its confluence with the Colorado River in Lake Mead.

INTRODUCTION

The Living Colorado River

A feather's not a bird
The rain is not the sea
A stone is not a mountain
But a river runs through me

—ROSANNE CASH

THERE'S A PLACE I LIKE TO GO not far up the Colorado River trail in Rocky Mountain National Park where the great river, maybe ten feet across, meanders through a subalpine meadow dotted with spruce and pine, the pointed peaks of the Never Summer Range poking into the sky. Here in the headwaters, the river gurgles softly most of the year, except during spring runoff, when it's a different river in a big rush to leave the mountains. I think about the river's journey, visualizing the contours of land and river course downstream, not so much the countless dams stair-stepping from every high place, impoundments powering the lives of forty million people, and canals stretching hundreds of miles, the waters of the massive storage system steadily dropping. Instead, I imagine six million years of continuous flow (until the 1960s) to the Colorado River Delta in the Gulf of California, a 1,450-mile river journey where everything, including us, is shaped by water. This meadow is a place to daydream, to whisper to the cow moose munching willow, to have a chat with chattering magpies, to be untroubled by declining snowpack and water shortages.

LEFT Like a feathered trout, an American dipper dives and probes for aquatic insects and insect larvae in Rocky Mountain National Park, Colorado. Dippers, North America's only aquatic songbird, inhabit turbulent, clear, fast-moving waters, diving underwater and thriving where streams and creeks tumble from the Rockies.

RIGHT An amber-colored glob of insect larvae plucked from the side of an instream boulder is a good catch for an American dipper, fishing the East Inlet Creek in Rocky Mountain National Park, Colorado.

PAGE 12 A clearing storm reveals the Never Summer Range headwaters of the Colorado River, with spring runoff spilling into the Kawuneeche Valley on the west side of Rocky Mountain National Park, Colorado.

As much as anything, I come here for solitude while admiring one of the awe-inspiring rivers of the world. With eyes shut, just listening, feeling, the scent of pine on a breeze, I'm transported to deep canyons where light barely pierces a fissure in stone, to the glassy river tongue entering roiling rapids like a watery mirror, to a cacophony of spring songbirds under a cool cottonwood canopy, to the miracle of water flowing over and through red desert stone. I mostly feel humility in these headwaters. This mighty river, humble yet determined, will go on to absorb tributary rivers—the Fraser, Eagle, Green, Gunnison, Dolores, Dirty Devil, Escalante, San Juan, Paria, Little Colorado, Gila—as she slices the Colorado Plateau, carves the Grand Canyon, carries life and hope in her flow, and feeds the nation from borderland industrial farms.

The Colorado and her tributaries sustain the miracle of migrating birds, many covering thousands of miles along the Central and Pacific Flyways. Tens of millions of birds migrate north in spring, billions of wing beats propelling avian rivers along the course of the Colorado. Some eighteen million birds migrate through the Colorado River Delta in Mexico and millions more up the San Pedro River in southeast

Arizona. Tens of thousands of sandhill cranes wintering in the borderlands touch our lives in communities and rest stops on their long journey north to the Yampa and upper Green Rivers. Trumpeter swans, North America's largest waterfowl species, have flown from Seedskadee National Wildlife Refuge in southwest Wyoming to the Grand Canyon and back, connecting most of the Colorado's watershed. When we see yellow warblers and broad-tailed hummingbirds in willow along headwaters streams, these diminutive birds have flown thousands of miles from Central and South America. We mark time by the arrival of these harbingers of spring, who will nest and raise their broods to make the long return to winter range in autumn, all of their movements driven by the need to perpetuate the species and the promise of good riparian habitat replete with cottonwood and willow.

Our wild brothers and sisters of the Colorado River watershed, bound to river flow and woody vegetation along the Colorado's main stem and far-reaching tributary arteries, have been aided by restoration and conservation stewards—river keepers—who are improving and creating habitat throughout the watershed. Replanting willow and cottonwood helps to restore ecosystem and riverine health and nurtures wildlife richness. Groundwater recharge beneath the San Pedro River in southeast Arizona gives life to more than four hundred wildlife species. Dredged, defined channels and replanted willow keep Colorado's Fraser River cool for trout and provide woody structure for

A wedge of trumpeter swans take flight in Seedskadee National Wildlife Refuge, Wyoming, between Fontenelle and Flaming Gorge Reservoirs along the Green River, the largest tributary of the Colorado River.

breeding songbirds here in the headwaters. With determination, ingenuity, and a stewardship ethos, experts and regular folks alike throughout the watershed are taking action to meet wildlife habitat needs while enhancing ecological health. Our collective engagement, riverine restoration projects, our stories and art and lifeways that shift our relationships to water in the West, the decision making that values the living river—all these endeavors are the collective voice for the mighty Colorado and the wild idea that healthy rivers benefit wildlife and people.

THE COLORADO RIVER STRETCHES FROM these headwaters in the Never Summer Range above the Kawuneeche Valley in Colorado's Rocky Mountain National Park to the Colorado River Delta on the Gulf of California in Mexico. Apart from a few outlier years since the 1960s, the river dries up in desert sand just over the Mexican border, but now a binational Raise the River Alliance restoration project is directing seasonal flow through a series of ditches in the Colorado floodplain to restore critical habitat and hope in the Delta.

If you include the river miles of the Colorado's major tributaries, all of those squiggly blue lines on maps quickly add up to thousands of river miles. Each of those tributary rivers is spectacular. Maps showing all of the rivers, streams, and creeks—the circulatory system of the watershed—look very much like the

After a night of roosting on shore ice, trumpeter swans drop into the icy main channel of the Green River in Seedskadee National Wildlife Refuge in southwest Wyoming. Seedskadee is a stronghold for North America's largest waterfowl species, which was nearly hunted to extinction for the plume trade in the late 1800s. Around three hundred individuals overwinter in the Green's open waters downstream from Fontenelle Reservoir.

veins and arteries of the human heart, or the human nervous system, or mycelium crawling across the forest floor, of life interconnected in river current. Flowing from all the high points that define its watershed basin, the Colorado drains 249,000 square miles and makes life possible from Denver to Los Angeles, from Salt Lake City to Yuma and to Mexicali and San Luis Rio Colorado, Mexico.

Still, there's no sugarcoating the peril of our water truth in the American West. Anyone reading these words has probably seen accounts of a dying Colorado River, the story of her decline told in images of cracked mud and white mineral bathtub rings marking historical high points around reservoirs. We collectively gasp while viewing small pools in Lake Powell and Lake Mead where boat ramps sink into desert sand, bemoaning dwindling snowpack and diminishing flows as gauges measure the declining amount of water flowing throughout the Colorado River Basin. Since 2000, extreme climate change–driven "megadrought" in the Interior West and Southwest has inflamed the gap between water allocation and actual "wet water" in the Colorado River system. The first-ever Declaration of Shortage on the Colorado River system, in 2021, followed by a tier-two shortage in August 2022, set off more alarms and triggered water allocation cuts in the Southwest, forecasting further and deeper cuts throughout the watershed. Spring through fall has become explosive wildfire season—for example, the autumn 2020 Troublesome Creek fire in the Colorado's headwaters region—when desiccated land is consumed by flames driven by hurricane-force winds, putting everyone on high alert. New research by scientists at University of California–

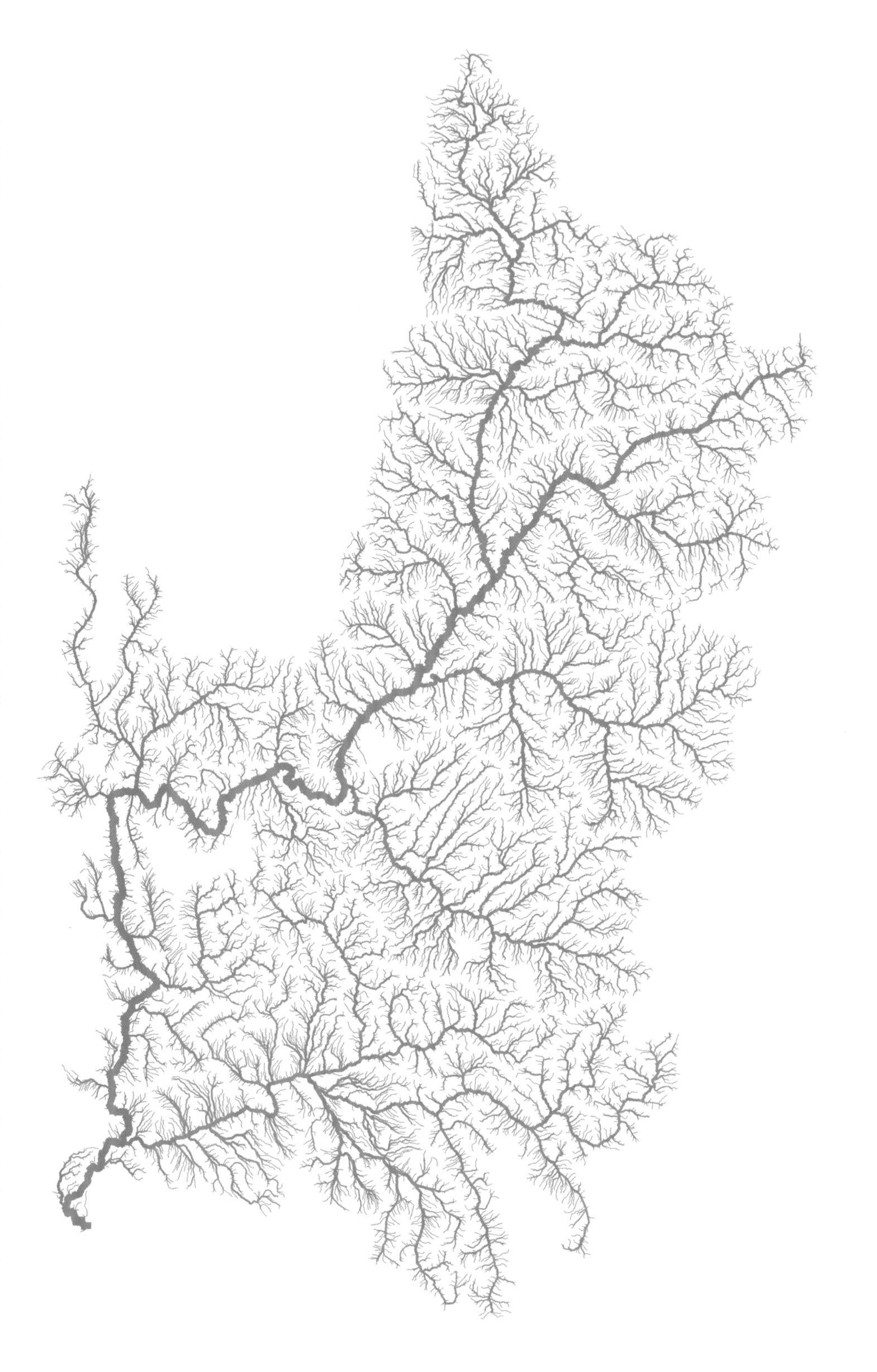

Los Angeles and Columbia University reported that the ongoing drought in the Colorado River Basin is the worst in twelve hundred years, with 42 percent of the severity driven by human-caused climate change.

The Colorado River is in crisis, yet she is still a flowing, living river. Eighty percent of her water is allocated to agriculture, most of which is used by the big borderland industrial agricultural producers, though agriculture is not monolithic. Imperial Valley, California, farming operations produce much of the nation's winter fruits and vegetables, and lettuce farms in Yuma, Arizona (which hold the highest-priority water rights in Arizona)—at the confluence of the Gila and the Colorado—grow 90 percent of the winter greens consumed in North America: when we eat a salad in winter, we are eating the Colorado River. These big borderland agricultural producers hold the most senior water rights in the watershed. Established by prior appropriation, generally water rights are considered "first in time, first in rights": in times of water shortage, senior water rights are fulfilled first, before later-appropriated "junior" water-rights holders can begin to use water tied to their rights.

"A river in crisis" makes for provocative headlines, yet all of this dire situation—which impacts forty million souls, resident and migrating birds, and all flora and fauna in the West—is a human construct and a decades-long failure to act. Journalists say, "The Colorado River is dying," but no, the river is not dying. The hard truth is that we waited too long to address the problem of systemic water shortage and are no longer able to deliver our water commitments to people, to agriculture, to fuel all of our wildest human ambitions everywhere in the arid American West. This oversimplified narrative of scarcity and competition for water also means that the river itself needs our collective voices for improving the watershed's resilience in the face of climate change, while sustaining an ever-expanding human population and a healthy, functioning river system. The Colorado River and her tributaries need more river keepers, folks with knowledge of and empathy for the river who are building a watershed community.

Color illustration of the entire Colorado River watershed's rivers and creeks. (Artwork by Robert Szucs/Grasshopper Geography)

RIVERS OF THE COLORADO RIVER WATERSHED are born in Colorado and Wyoming, when the high Rocky Mountain peaks release snowmelt over a miraculous couple of months in spring, when flowing water is everywhere in the alpine—dripping from snowfields, racing down mountainsides, roaring through constricted canyons to valleys below. In early spring, our water year has already been measured in snowpack depth and water content by aerial surveys and sensors strategically placed throughout the Rockies, and by April, water users in watersheds of the Colorado (as well as the neighboring Rio Grande, the Platte, the Arkansas, and many more) know their water future for another season.

The waters of the Colorado River are still allocated by the antiquated 1922 Colorado River Compact, which divided the watershed at Lees Ferry, Arizona, into Upper and Lower Basins: the Upper Basin states are Colorado, Wyoming, Utah, and New Mexico; Lower Basin states are Nevada, Arizona, and California. In January 1922, with then secretary of commerce Herbert Hoover as chairman of the Colorado River Commission, delegates of the seven Colorado River Basin states met to discuss how to allocate the waters of the

Colorado under this interstate compact but were unable to agree—and most of those states feared faster-growing California would establish senior priority rights. Even after six states reached an interstate compact agreement later that year, Arizona contested the Compact, refused to sign, and delayed its ratification of the Compact until 1944.

The collaborative document that emerged in November 1922 pushed aside good hydrologic science, favoring the most optimistic estimates of water in the Colorado River. The Colorado River Compact's allocation data favored wet years and overestimated the watershed's available flow at around 18 million acre-feet (maf). An acre-foot of water is one foot deep over one acre—about a football field one foot deep—which is roughly enough water today to support two typical households for a year. The Compact designated an annual allocation of 7.5 maf to the Upper Basin and 7.5 maf (8.5 maf with additional flows) to the Lower Basin (obligating the Upper Basin to allow an average of 75 maf in a ten-year rolling average to pass Lees Ferry) without acknowledging the loss of another 1.5 maf a year to evaporation. A little over two decades later, another 1.5 maf of Colorado water was allocated to Mexico with the signing of the 1944 US-Mexico Water Treaty regarding utilization of waters of the Colorado, Tijuana, and Rio Grande Rivers. The arithmetic will make one's eyes glaze over, but the Lower Basin's allocation of 8.5 maf and Mexico's 1.5 maf, together with the Upper Basin's present use of about 4.5 maf and another 1.5 maf of evaporation, all adds up to about 16 maf. But even these allocations have turned out to be overoptimistic.

IN 1922, WHEN THE COMBINED POPULATIONS OF Los Angeles, Denver, Phoenix, and Las Vegas totaled fewer than one million people, no one could foresee that forty million people would come to depend on the Colorado, but our current quandary is also linked to excessive optimism in the dam-building era and possibly a myopic disregard for river health and available flows. All this occurred when plans for a chain of dams to control the river laid the foundations for a new opening of the West. The Colorado River is often called "the world's hardest-working river," not only because the same water is used and reused over and over as it moves downstream but also because of the remarkable infrastructure, or plumbing system, that delivers water to forty million people and to industrialized agriculture that feeds the nation. Downstream from the Grand Canyon, the Colorado is impounded behind a string of dams—Hoover (creating Lake Mead), Davis (Lake Mohave), Parker (Lake Havasu), Imperial, and Morelos on the Mexican border. Originating at Lake Havasu behind Parker Dam are the Colorado River Aqueduct, which diverts water 250 miles to the Coachella Valley and Los Angeles, and the 336-mile-long Central Arizona Project (CAP), which makes modern life possible in Phoenix and Tucson.

While these feats of human engineering are indeed remarkable, and part of the Colorado River story, they have ultimately led to over-allocation, overuse, and the draining of a six-million-year-old river in one century. In recent years, flow past the Lees Ferry gauge has averaged about 12.47 maf and continues trending down—still with 16 maf appropriated. The simple truth in all of this math is there is less water in our rivers, and the gap between water allocation and how much water we have is growing. Conservation can help close the gap, and cuts are inevitable.

The science of actual river flow existed in 1922. *Science Be Dammed* by Eric Kuhn and John Fleck introduces United States Geological Survey hydrologist E. C. LaRue, who addressed a 1925 US Senate hearing: "'The flow of the Colorado River and its tributaries,' LaRue told the senators, 'is not sufficient to irrigate all the irrigable lands lying within the basin.'" Fleck later blogged that "LaRue's cautions came fully three years before Congress ratified the compact and plunged us headlong into decades of dam and canal building that overshot the amount of water the Colorado River had to fill them."

TOP Wheel-line irrigation and golden autumn cottonwoods line the Colorado River near Westwater, on the Colorado-Utah state line.

BOTTOM Near the bottom of the Colorado's watershed, the Yuma industrial lettuce farms grow 90 percent of all winter greens in North America. When we eat a salad in winter, we are eating the Colorado River. The Yuma lettuce producers have the highest-priority water rights in the state of Arizona.

Dubbed the "Las Vegas sundial," and also a water gauge of sorts, a 1960s speedboat in Government Wash was revealed in Lake Mead as waters receded over a number of months in the spring of 2022. The boat was once under 150 feet of water; the ridges encircling the bay were also inundated. When the image was made in the summer of 2022, Lake Mead, the largest US reservoir and water storage for the Lower Basin states and Mexico, was at 27 percent of capacity.

The 1922 Colorado River Compact is also the foundation of the Law of the River, an aggregate of compacts, federal laws, court decisions, decrees, contracts, and regulatory guidelines determining how the waters of the Colorado River are used. The collaborative aspect of the hundred-year-old Compact lends stability and a history of comity for future negotiations among the seven basin states, although water rights of twenty-six federally recognized tribes on twenty-nine reservations in the Colorado watershed were largely excluded. The 2026 expiration of the existing river management guidelines has sparked a renegotiation process—a reckoning with climate change, reduced snowpack, settling of tribal water rights, and systemic water shortages. Renegotiation of the Compact guidelines, which affects a river flowing through two countries, the land of thirty Indigenous tribes, and seven states, provides an opportunity to make access to the Colorado's water equitable as well as sustainable—for instance, some inclusion of the Ten Tribes Partnership in discussions indicates progress.

No one knows how low the river flow will be in the coming years, or how much river runoff will be absorbed by desiccated soil, but climate science indicates that flow from mountain snowpack will continue to decline in the decades ahead. Because we waited decades to act on climate-driven water shortages exacerbated by overallocation, some of the coming reductions will seem draconian, and they will be shared by all who rely on Colorado River water. There's no getting around the notion that how we use water must change—and is changing now. The major cities in the watershed—Denver, Salt Lake City, Albuquerque, Las Vegas, Phoenix, Tucson, San Diego, and Los Angeles—have proven their ability to reduce water consumption below levels of twenty years ago while continuing to grow: a hopeful signal with major cuts on the horizon.

But meaningful water conservation is only one step toward a fundamental change in our relationship to water in the West. This story about the Colorado River watershed, its natural history and life-giving promise, is essentially about our relationship to the great river. Restoring our relationship with water in the West begins with asking, Where does our water come from? And who does it connect us to? In our relationships as downstream watershed neighbors, in

Commuters travel Interstate 25, backed by the Denver skyline, during evening rush hour. About 50 percent of Denver's water comes from the Colorado River collection system via the Moffat Water Tunnel, a transmountain diversion of the Fraser River, and the Blue River impounded at Dillon Reservoir in Summit County.

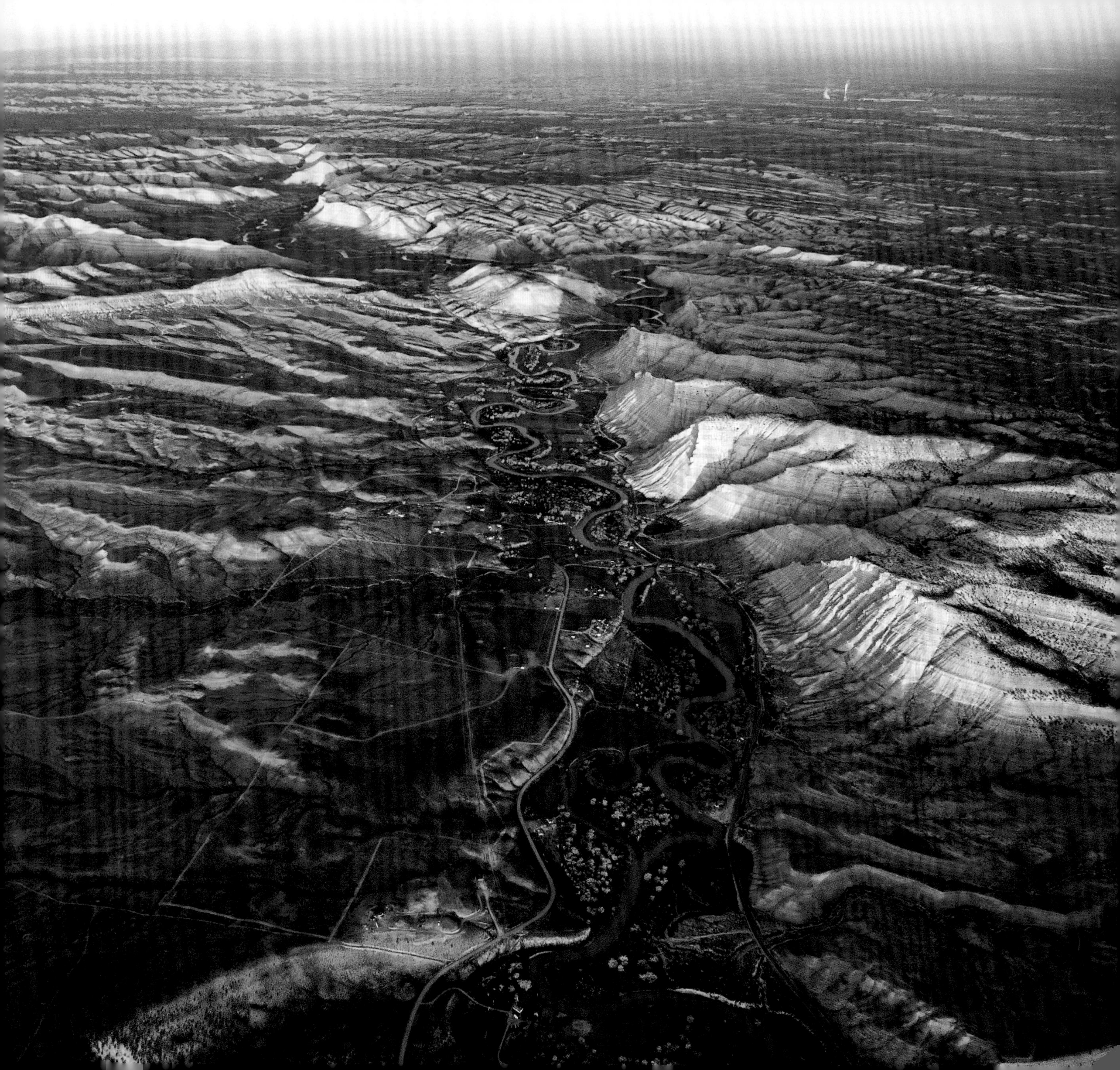

OPPOSITE The White River stretches to the west in this view near Rangley, Colorado. The 195-mile-long White River begins in Colorado's Flattop Wilderness and joins the Green River south of Vernal, Utah. (LightHawk aerial support)

TOP The Central Arizona Project (CAP) canal travels through the north Phoenix area; Lake Pleasant, in the background, is the CAP storage reservoir, impounding Colorado River and Agua Fria river water. The CAP runs 336 miles from Lake Havasu, on the California–Arizona state line, to Tucson, Arizona. (LightHawk aerial support)

BOTTOM Above the city of Aspen, Colorado, snowcats high on the slopes, headlights glowing, groom Aspen Mountain ski area. With climate change shrinking ski seasons, Aspen Skiing Company and Colorado Ski Country USA resorts use sustainability programs with renewable energy and snowmaking efficiency to mitigate impacts.

TOP A golden cottonwood leaf settles onto cracked mud in the streambed of ephemeral Mogollon (muggy-OWN) Creek in the Mogollon Box, Gila Riparian Preserve, New Mexico.

BOTTOM Cottonwoods, with a tinge of emerging lime-green spring leaves, mark the Escalante River channel in Grand Staircase–Escalante National Monument, Utah. The ninety-mile-long Escalante meets the Colorado at Lake Powell.

knowing and loving our rivers, is the genesis of hope for a healthy Colorado River watershed.

Nature still decides how much water we have in spring snowpack, and incremental water savings won't erase a systemic gap in allocation and supply. Hope for more snow is not a strategy. The question isn't whether we're using less water but whether we're doing all we can watershed-wide to leverage demand and to protect supply and the wild heart of the Colorado River. Why do we still irrigate lawns in the arid West? Do we talk about crop mix and take a hard look at water-intensive crops like alfalfa and cotton? How large a role does demand management—the temporary, voluntary, and compensated practice of fallowing farm fields and returning water to the river—play in balancing demand with supply? No one wants their allocations cut, yet as Ted Kowalski of the Walton Family Foundation told me, "There are no silver bullets." We'll be drinking purified gray water, tearing out lawns, and fallowing farm fields to continue living in the watershed of the Colorado. It will take courage to keep our rivers flowing for the benefit of wildlife and people, to see our lives tethered to her wild promise, and to change our very relationship to rivers.

A CONFLUENCE OF EVENTS LED ME TO THIS river story at a time when I wasn't looking for a long-term project. My wife, Marla Ofstad, and I had been exploring the watershed for decades, reaching summits of Colorado fourteeners, adventuring below the rim of the Grand Canyon, backpacking the alpine headwaters in the Never Summers, Elks, and San Juans, and rolling over mountain passes revealing endless vistas where rivulets and streams burble, gaining power and roiling through the forested valleys below. We'd witnessed snowpack decreasing in real time, alpine tundra grasses turning crispy when snow should still be lingering, just by wandering high in the mountains.

I'd also been working with friends and colleagues Mike Forsberg and Mike Farrell, cofounders of the Platte Basin Timelapse, for a number of years. An in-depth long-term watershed study, PBT uses time-lapse photography and multimedia storytelling to help people understand what it means to live in a watershed today. PBT is made up of a diverse team of producers, engineers, researchers, and students based out of the University of Nebraska–Lincoln. Through the work of talented young PBT producers and time in the presence of the great sandhill crane migration on the Platte River at Audubon's Rowe Sanctuary and around Kearney, Nebraska, as well as studying rivers through the seasons, I came to see myself as part of a broader watershed conservation community, where compelling imagery and stories have the power to change perspectives. Then, while presenting at the 2015 Audubon Society National Meeting in Leesburg, Virginia, I attended a breakout session of the Western Rivers Action Network, a collaborative, layered, and far-reaching conservation campaign built on the simple premise that "healthy rivers benefit wildlife and people." In that moment, with conservation leaders engaged throughout the watershed of the Colorado, I thought I could possibly contribute by telling this story.

My first field expedition intended for this book—and the first raft trip of my life—was with coleaders Alison Holloran and Abby Burk of Audubon Rockies on a float trip in Dinosaur National Monument down the

free-flowing but imperiled Yampa River, a major tributary of the Green River from Colorado's northwest corner into Utah. Quickly, after a few big, soaking rapids, we *were* the river. We floated under impossibly tall golden canyon walls, streaked by desert varnish and time, finding a rhythm in the current, in beauty unfolding around each river bend, in solitude of ephemeral camps under a nightfall of diamonds. Two more raft trips with Audubon Rockies followed, one down the length of the Grand Canyon and another through Utah's Cataract Canyon and Big Drops One, Two, and Three from Moab to the Hite launch on the northern end of Lake Powell. Each expedition was a gift of adventure, camaraderie, lore, beauty, soulful introspection, a shared connectedness and responsibility to rivers and downstream neighbors.

In those first few years I set out to see most of the watershed, to take in the breadth of a beloved and imperiled river system. LightHawk, a conservation flying nonprofit, took me high above the majestic Wind River Range glaciers at the head of the Green River in Greater Yellowstone where rivers are born, then Marla and I backpacked to the headwaters. Downstream, Seedskadee National Wildlife Refuge felt like a classically western home with the Green River flowing through historical ranch land and arid Little Colorado Desert sage. Situated below the northernmost dam—Fontenelle—in the Colorado River system, the refuge is

OARS raft guide Dave Garcia navigates a dory through the Big Drops in Cataract Canyon while Silencia Cox steadies herself through the powerful rapids. Cataract Canyon was named by John Wesley Powell on the first exploration of the Colorado River through the Grand Canyon, in 1869.

steadily restoring riverine habitat where the impoundment obstructs spring floods that had nurtured new cottonwood and willow growth, woody foundations of wildlife richness and healthy rivers. In spite of our capacity to alter river flow and bend the land to our will, Seedskadee supports abundant wildlife and world-class fishing where the Green River's ribbon of blue is the lifeblood of southwest Wyoming.

Presence or absence of cottonwood and willow, diminishing snowpack, effects of dams and diversions, desiccated land, wildfire threats, and unyielding pressure on a finite water supply are convergent themes revealed throughout the watershed. So are collaborative conservation and our collective proclivity for habitat restoration. In the headwaters where the Colorado leaves Rocky Mountain National Park, and where the Fraser River makes a thirty-two-mile run to its confluence with the Colorado, declining snowpack and runoff, major diversions to Denver, and explosive wildfire mark changes of season. Yet there is life in flow and hope in collaboration where Trout Unlimited, Colorado Parks and Wildlife, and Denver Water are engaged in

In a kayak readying to lead a Yampa River raft trip, Abby Burk, manager of Audubon Rockies' Western Rivers Regional Program, says, "I've been bound by the wonder of water and the connection of rivers my whole life." Here, on the Yampa in Dinosaur National Monument, Utah, Abby adds, "There is an inseparable connection of water and rivers to my life . . . it's a unique language of vivid and rich watery impressions that engage all senses. . . . Simply put, I am enamored by water, and the love of rivers drives my life."

White birds symbolize peace, hope, and purity across many cultures, and the white-tailed ptarmigan is North America's white bird of the high alpine. This brilliant white ptarmigan feather in Colorado's Arapaho National Forest gave me pause to study the intimate beauty in a square foot of tundra grass, autumn colors underfoot in an immense mountain landscape atop the Continental Divide in the Fraser River headwaters. Moments after viewing the feather, my wife, Marla Ofstad, spotted a ptarmigan hen with three chicks, almost adult size—hope on the cusp of a new snow year.

Grand County Learning by Doing Cooperative Effort projects for the health of the Fraser River. A decades-old idea to enhance river health resulted in construction of the Windy Gap bypass in fall 2022 to create a channel around the reservoir impounding the mainstem Colorado in the headwaters, which will maintain stream integrity, increase aquatic insects and sculpin, and allow fish to move freely up and down the channel.

On the upper Gila River in southwest New Mexico, climate change is attacking snowpack in the Mogollon (muggy-OWN) Mountain headwaters while explosive wildfires burn vast swaths of wilderness. Yet a decades-long dispute over a dam and diversion of the upper Gila's water to Arizona was shelved in 2021, and today the Gila is a wild and free river through its headwaters. The Nature Conservancy's Martha Cooper is integral to community-based conservation work on the upper Gila, which today is a reference river for the possible and treasured by those who know these legendary waters.

The San Pedro River in southeast Arizona, depleted by four decades of unfettered groundwater pumping, is both a critically important river for wildlife and migrating birds breeding in the northern hemisphere and totally reliant on groundwater recharge to have flowing surface water support riverine health and human life in the basin around Sierra Vista, Arizona. Equal parts visionary and community organizer, Holly Richter of The Nature Conservancy engages the Sierra

Vista community in studying the San Pedro while lending her expertise in mapping and recharging groundwater for river health.

I focused on these places for their beauty, conservation stories, remarkable characters, imperiled species, regional emblematic nature, and import to the Colorado's whole watershed. The same challenges resurfaced, laid bare by knowing there is much less water in the entire system.

MY WATERSHED VIEW SHIFTED MOST WHEN I ATTENDED the 2019 Utah Diné Bikéyah Summer Gathering in Bears Ears National Monument, where the Bears Ears Inter-Tribal Coalition gathered. People of the Hopi Tribe, Navajo Nation, Ute Mountain Ute Tribe, Pueblo of Zuni, and Ute Indian Tribe—the coalition—generously invited folks to join, learn, and strengthen the extended Bears Ears community that is the cultural and spiritual center for Indigenous people with deep ancestral roots in sacred Bears Ears.

Later I met Cynthia Wilson, director of the Utah Diné Bikéyah Traditional Foods Program, and her beautiful family in Monument Valley, Utah, where I gained valuable perspective into life without access to clean water, which affects nearly half of Indigenous households. Simply traveling to and hauling clean water is high on the list of daily challenges Indigenous people face, and the US government has failed in the promise of its treaties for a permanent livable homeland, which in tribal lands without access to clean water is only a mirage. The US Departments of Agriculture and Interior recently developed the Tribal Homelands Initiative to "strengthen Tribal co-stewardship of public lands and waters." The initiative "will incorporate Tribal capacity, expertise, and Indigenous knowledge into federal land and resources management." Progress was made in 2021 with the introduction of the Tribal Access to Clean Water Act, which also would appropriate infrastructure funding. These meaningful actions, with new funding through the bipartisan infrastructure law and tribal comanagement of Bears Ears National Monument, are positive steps toward addressing systemic inequity in water access and managing our public lands.

I am grateful for the generosity and kindness of all the Indigenous people I've met through Utah Diné Bikéyah and am inspired by their dignity in culture, family, community, native language, and a deep spiritual connection to the natural world. I've also learned from my Indigenous friends that the Colorado is a female river, as brought to life beautifully in Cynthia Wilson's essay in the Bears Ears chapter.

Bears Ears National Monument's southern boundary abuts the San Juan River, which joins the Colorado at Lake Powell. Passing through a half dozen big dams and the Grand Canyon, the Colorado River now is flowing in its delta with water allocated for restoration, and the binational Raise the River Alliance is collaborating to restore 2,300 acres of critical habitat for people, birds, and wildlife.

Over the past six years, my relationship to the waters of the Colorado River has grown into something akin to visiting a dear friend. I've developed a ritual of squatting next to her current and dipping my cupped hands into her icy waters, then soaking my face while telling the river I love her. Before writing this book, I went to the river and asked her to flow through me so I could tell her story. I do this now in all her tributaries too, the arteries of the mighty river that makes life possible in the arid West. I come here to ponder the river's intention, a purity of purpose to simply flow downstream and to carry in her current a soul of life—all life, however connected to her force.

Hope and love are more powerful emotions than despair. There's no giving up on the Colorado in this story, this river, and these river keepers. There is less water in the Colorado River system than at any time in recorded history, yet in my experience, wherever there is water and flow, there is life—abundant, dynamic life. Hope lives in these people who are collaborating and doing great work for a resilient watershed. I am compelled to tell a story of the Living River in hopes more people will engage, care, and see themselves reflected in the great river. As we become part of an extended watershed community bound by love, hope, reverence, and rivers flowing through each of us, we are the river.

Blooming lupine carpet a high alpine meadow in a setting of lime-green spring leaves and 13,496-foot Mears Peak in the San Juan Mountains, ancestral homelands of the Ute people, in the Uncompahgre National Forest, Colorado.

LAND ACKNOWLEDGMENT

ALL UNITED STATES LANDS ARE ANCESTRAL HOMELANDS. A "land acknowledgment," or "territorial acknowledgment," is a formal statement that recognizes the unique and enduring relationship that exists between Indigenous peoples and their traditional territories and commemorates the fact that Indigenous people have not and cannot be erased. Here is my land acknowledgment:

I acknowledge that I live and work in the ancestral homelands of the Apache, Arapaho, Cheyenne, Comanche, and Ute peoples. I also acknowledge that while in the Bears Ears region, I work in the ancestral homelands of Hopi, Navajo, Ute, Ute Mountain Ute, and Zuni peoples and, throughout the watershed of the Colorado, the ancestral homelands of thirty North American Indigenous tribes. I understand that these lands hold enormous sacred, cultural, and spiritual significance for their original stewards, the Indigenous peoples of the Colorado River region.

I asked Angelo Baca, coordinator of cultural resources for Utah Diné Bikéyah, a nonprofit organization dedicated to the defense and protection of culturally significant ancestral lands, about Indigenous tribes and land acknowledgment.

Angelo said, "Indigenous peoples see themselves and the land as one. Each cannot be separated from the other; if you see the landscape, then you see me; if you see me, then you see my landscape. This is what a real land acknowledgment looks like:"

Angelo Baca yinishe
Tlaaschchi'i' Nishlii
Keesani Bashishchine
To'dichini da Shicheii
Nakaii Dinée' da Shinali

Translation: Hello. My name is Angelo Baca. My clans are the Red Bottom People, Hope People, Bitter Water, and Mexican People Clans. ✲

DR. ANGELO BACA is a cultural activist, scholar, teacher, filmmaker, and recently graduated doctoral student in anthropology at New York University, with a certificate in the Culture and Media documentary film program. The National Parks Conservation Association designated him as one of "10 Under 40" dynamic cultural activists who made up the association's Next Generation Advisory Council in 2018. He has published widely read opinion essays in the *New York Times*, *Outside* magazine, and the *Salt Lake City Tribune*. Baca's latest award-winning film, *Shash Jaa': Bears Ears*, is about the five tribes of the Bears Ears Inter-Tribal Coalition that worked together to protect 1.9 million acres of Utah wilderness through a national monument designation, which eventually resulted in the 1.35-million-acre Obama-era designation. His work reflects a long-standing dedication to both Western and Indigenous knowledge, as well as to Indigenous representation, voices, and narrative foregrounding, including building collaborative partnerships of environmental and outdoor groups with Indigenous nations on equal and respectful grounds.

EARTH'S BREATH: INSPIRATION IN BIRD MIGRATION

BY ALISON HOLLORAN

BIRD MIGRATION—IT IS THE VISIBLE BREATH and life of the planet. As if pushed by a long exhale, birds ride the planet's winds from as far away as South America, finding their way north to their breeding grounds in spring, many contained within the wetlands and cottonwood galleries lining the mighty Colorado River, then back south to their wintering grounds in fall. In spring, when the earth is ready to renew, it seems as if birds bring it all to life through migration—eager travelers searching for new and familiar places to spend the critical summer months. These migrations are essential to many birds' survival, offering replenished food sources and safe places to raise their young.

While the winds help carry the birds, the rivers, wetlands, and lakes of the Colorado River Basin are the network of riverine veins and arteries that help sustain the birds during their tenuous migrations. These waters are the lifeblood that pumps across the earth, providing the "oxygen" needed for these great migrations.

Two bird species in particular articulate the complex and delicate breath of migration: the yellow warbler and the sandhill crane. Let me start with the smaller of my two "friends." I know yellow warblers well. Running a banding station (at these stations, birds are fitted with leg bands so we may better understand where they go and what obstacles they may face, as well as to gauge survival rates) for almost two decades has given me the privilege of holding their tiny bodies, feeling their rapid heartbeats, taking in the beauty of their extraordinary colors. As I hold them, it boggles my mind to think about where they have come from, the many thousands of miles they cover, and the habitat

they need to make their journeys—not once, but twice, every year. This *tiny* bird, at most five inches long and weighing less than half an ounce (so small they can sometimes get caught in a spider's web), starts its northward journey from places as distant as northern South America to spend warm summers in the cottonwoods and willows along the river edges throughout the Colorado River Basin and beyond.

How do the warblers do it? How do they find the stamina and strength on a migration filled with long days and cold nights? They rely on what flourishes in the rivers' habitats: critical food like protein-packed insects and, for shelter, the dense network of limbs, twigs, and leaves that only the plant life near rivers can provide for these tiny travelers. I have come to think of these birds as my treasured friends, and I am happy to see them back each year, knowing they have safely returned once again to spend their summer here, allowing me to be a witness of their journey.

Migration does not discriminate. Big or small, fast or slow, many birds are called to move, to breathe with the earth. Some birds make a first impression you will never forget. It was while working on my master's research in Pinedale, Wyoming, that I first heard the sandhill cranes' call. They had worked their way north from New Mexico or maybe Texas through snowstorms and cold winds, stopping in icy rivers for a quick meal and rest, only to take flight again each dawn, continuing north, some into Canada, to mate and raise their young. Lying in my bed just after sunrise, I listened as the cranes flew low over my house, headed for the marshy wetlands and the nearby river, calling to their companions and mates. The first time I heard them I ran out of the house, wondering what they could be, their vocalizations so beautiful. Some describe the cranes' call as sounding like a trumpet, but that seems too abrupt, too loud; to me, they sound like they are quietly talking to one another, low and soft, consistent, not tired or angry but offering support and hope during their long journey together.

After hearing the cranes' song, I was able to follow the birds throughout the summer. I watched them dance and build nests. I collected some of their feathers as they molted, readying themselves to follow the river back south to their wintering grounds. I put their feathers in my hat, wanting to carry them with me wherever I went (twenty-plus years later, I still have a few of those feathers). The birds and I both departed late that summer. I made a "short" trip of 300 miles back to the university, and the cranes

Alison Holloran, executive director of Audubon Rockies, along the Cache la Poudre River near her Fort Collins, Colorado, home

PAGE 34 A brilliant male yellow warbler sings from restored willow along Colorado's Fraser River while defending breeding territory in May. The willow along Fraser Flats was transplanted by volunteers from nearby Ranch Creek as part of a Grand County Learning by Doing Cooperative Effort project.

PAGE 35 A mountain bluebird perches in front of its nest hole in a gnarled aspen tree on a mountainside in the Bridger–Teton Wilderness, in the Green River headwaters.

Sandhill cranes take flight in waves from their overnight roost to feed in agricultural fields and wetlands. Here, ponds are flooded ankle deep to provide a roost, and the cranes respond in big numbers. More than forty-five thousand sandhill cranes of the Rocky Mountain and Central Flyway flocks gather in southeast Arizona's Sulphur Springs Valley in winter.

began their long journey of many more hundreds of miles following the twisting veins of the Green River, the Colorado River's chief tributary.

The cranes, warblers, and other birds are part of the earth's breath—that is how I see them, how they inspire me. Moving up and down the river corridors, birds are a litmus test. Their presence or absence, abundance, and ability to raise another generation tell us how we are doing in conserving their home, our home. I find myself standing very still in the early spring, listening for their songs, hoping to hear them tell me they are back on another deep breath. ✲

Audubon Rockies Executive Director **ALISON HOLLORAN** grew up exploring the woods and seashores of Maryland before earning a bachelor of science degree in wildlife management at West Virginia University and a masters of zoology and physiology from the University of Wyoming. Before her twenty-plus-year Audubon career, Alison worked for the Peace Corps in Honduras and studied the potential effects of oil and gas development on greater sage-grouse in Sublette County, Wyoming. Alison lives in Fort Collins, Colorado, with her husband, Matt, and their two daughters. The Hollorans are an avid conservation and rafting family with a love of western rivers.

LEFT Between six hundred and twelve hundred sandhill cranes spend breeding season in the Yampa River valley. Here, this individual is harassed by a red-winged blackbird in Yampa River backwaters near Steamboat Springs, Colorado.

RIGHT After a morning of feeding in pasture grass, a pair of sandhill cranes trace the upper Gila River upstream with an autumn backdrop of golden cottonwood and orange sycamore. A small population of sandhill cranes, most likely of the Rocky Mountain flock, use the upper Gila headwaters for winter range before migrating north in February.

OPPOSITE An impressive desert bighorn sheep ram in Colorado National Monument (CNM) near Fruita and Grand Junction in Colorado's Grand Valley. Desert bighorns, which have adapted to hot, dry climates, were once in danger of extinction; the CNM herd was reintroduced in 1979 with animals from the Lake Mead area.

TOP This apparent bighorn sheep pictograph with young and a human figure is found on canyon walls along the Yampa River in Dinosaur National Monument, Utah, originally inhabited by the ancestral Ute people.

BOTTOM Juvenile desert bighorn sheep roam the sagebrush uplands of CNM above the Colorado River. Historically, about 1.5 to 2 million bighorn sheep roamed North America. Today, the total population is around 49,000. Diseases transmitted by domestic sheep are among the major threats to sustainable bighorn sheep recovery.

While I hiked up Angels Landing in Utah's Zion National Park, two adult California condors and one black-headed juvenile lifted from a cliff face, flying several rapid circles overhead before disappearing as swiftly as they'd appeared. This adult is female 409 (tag 9), who with male 523 (tag J3) successfully hatched chick No. 1000 in 2019 and No. 1111 in 2021. Lead poisoning from scavenging animals killed with lead bullets remains the biggest threat to the endangered condors, and lead-free ammunition is available at no cost in Utah during hunting season.

OPPOSITE Fireweed in bloom lines the shores of Wall Lake, one of many alpine lakes that form the headwaters of the Yampa River high in Colorado's Flattop Wilderness.

OPPOSITE The desert varnish–streaked Tiger Wall along the Yampa River in Dinosaur National Monument, Utah, is a stunning sight with an interesting legend—it is said that if you kiss the Tiger Wall, you'll have safe passage through the rapids downstream.

LEFT Spectacular Buckskin Canyon has been carved by Buckskin Creek, a major tributary of the Paria River, into one of the longest and deepest slot canyons in the world. In the sandstone canyon near Kanab, Utah, I found myself continually looking up at giant logs wedged in the narrow slot—remnants of flash floods that continue to shape canyons of the Southwest. The Paria River joins the Colorado River just downstream from Lees Ferry in Glen Canyon National Recreation Area.

TOP Colorful collared lizards, commonly seen in Dominguez Canyons Wilderness on the edge of the Uncompahgre Plateau, range throughout the Southwest, feeding on insects and other lizards.

BOTTOM Mount Garfield's summit view overlooks the Grand Valley (the Colorado was originally called the Grand River) and the farms of Palisade, sandwiched between the Colorado River and Interstate 70 near Grand Junction in western Colorado. At the head of the valley is Grand Mesa, at more than 10,000 feet elevation the largest flattop mountain in the world. The Grand Valley is a major recreation hub and agricultural region known for peaches, cherries, corn, wine grapes, hay, and other crops.

OPPOSITE Big Dominguez Creek plunges through 1.5-billion-year-old Precambrian rock to its meeting with the Gunnison River a few miles downstream. Dominguez Canyons Wilderness, Colorado, remains an important cultural connection for the Ute people, who for more than a millennia have traveled along the perennial stream corridor between the Uncompahgre Plateau and the Gunnison River.

PAGE 48 The Salton Sea, sandwiched between the Coachella Valley to the north and the Imperial Valley to the south, is an imperiled inland playa lake. The modern Salton Sea was created by an accidental levee break in 1905 that released Colorado River water into the lakebed for two years before the break was repaired. Today, the lake is highly polluted and shrinking, with extremely high salinity levels, yet it is still a designated Important Bird Area in the Pacific Flyway. One proposal to save the Salton Sea and protect residents in surrounding towns from toxic blowing dust is a 160-mile pipeline from the Gulf of California in Mexico.

Constructed from 1931 to 1936, Hoover Dam controlled floods of the mighty Colorado River, provides irrigation water for Southwest agriculture, and generates hydroelectric power. The dam's dimensions are staggering: 726 feet high, 1,244 feet long, and 660 feet thick at its base. Behind Hoover Dam, Lake Mead serves primarily as storage for the Lower Basin states of California, Nevada, and Arizona, as well as Mexico. Lake Mead, last full in 1983 as marked by white bathtub-ring high-water marks in Boulder Canyon, was at 27 percent capacity when this image was made in the summer of 2022.

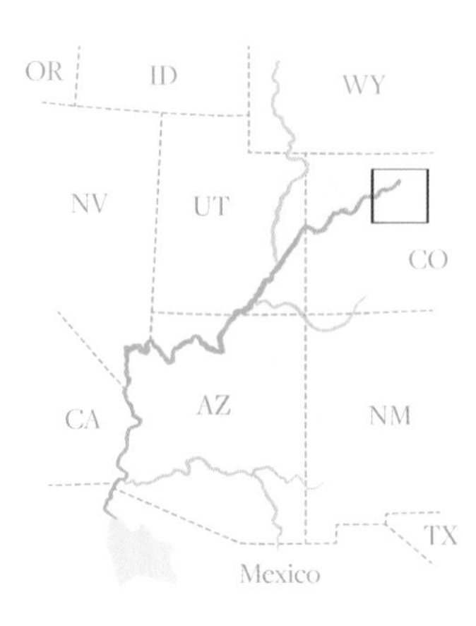

Chapter 1

HEADWATERS

Straddling the Continental Divide

IN LAST LIGHT ON THE LAST NIGHT OF WINTER, anticipating a full moon, we stood atop the rounded summit of James Peak, at 13,294 feet the high point of the Southern Rockies' broad-shouldered Front Range, which divides the Fraser River valley on the Colorado River side and the city of Boulder and the Denver metro area on the Platte River side. We had been blown off a handful of times that season in our quest to reach the summit in winter and stubbornly returned for one last push. Each attempt began at the base of Saint Marys Glacier on the Platte side—not a glacier but a large permanent snowfield that melts into South Boulder Creek, which tumbles and flows to the city of Boulder. The steep snowfield was windblown and crunchy, with encrusted waves of sastrugi snow in spots, easy going on traction spikes with fair winds and sunshine. The constricted point just before the summit pitch is often the crux where progress and fun both vanish in the wind, but passage to James's summit was clear this day.

In burly down parkas, my wife, Marla, friend Marc Flink, and I studied each ridge and feature of so many craggy and rounded summits before us, all leading to distant Longs Peak, at more than 14,000 feet on the Rocky Mountain National Park skyline. We wondered if the supermoon would show through low clouds over the plains as my thoughts turned to the idea that the snowpack beneath our feet and laid out before us was all the water we would have for the next year. When it all melts, some will reach the Mississippi River via the Platte and Missouri, while the Colorado will flow to Mexico and stretch west to Los Angeles via 250 miles of diversion pipes and pumping stations. This moment became a turning point, when I began thinking seriously about water in the American West.

Blue and white of dusk and snowfields faded to gray, and the lights of Denver and Boulder began twinkling on the eastern horizon as we descended into darkness, three headlamp cones reflecting a few square yards of snow in the massive blue-black landscape. Clouds thinned, moonlight revealing familiar details in the alpine basin and enough footprints from the hike up to mark our descent route. Colorful lights of the megalopolis bounced off a faraway cloud bank, and I felt a sense of purity in this singular experience wrapped in solitude, lingering moments of three tiny figures crunching down a mountain under a cold moon in the deepest of blues. We found our way to cars, pizza, and home, some 7,500 vertical feet beneath James's summit.

Home is Arvada, a western Denver suburb that still holds charming remnants of its horse-ranching heyday. Twenty years ago, it was common to be slowed by a tractor while driving city streets. It's a desirable place to live for the climate, renowned school system, and proximity to the Front Range and Colorado's iconic Rocky Mountain wonderland. Layers of new developments stretch to within a few miles of the foothills, each home with its attendant bluegrass lawn, emerald green well into October. It's a bucolic suburban setting of greenbelt bike paths, wetland ponds, and reservoirs dotting the prairie. A high foothills view reveals a landscape defined more by water storage and conveyance than its shortgrass prairie natural history. In arid Denver and the surrounding suburbs, you can water your lawn every day of summer, if you please. New people keep coming, and subdivisions pop up so quickly now that it's hard to remember when they were raised.

Although Arvada and the entire Denver metro area are situated east of the Rockies in the South Platte River watershed, all of our lives on the Front Range are built on Colorado River water, diverted from her Fraser River tributary at the Winter Park Resort ski area. The Moffat Water Tunnel, a ten-foot-diameter bore, runs 6.2 miles from Winter Park through the Rocky Mountains—beneath our feet where we stood on James Peak. In a line north to south from Winter Park, water diverted from the Rockies' Western Slope to Denver flows through miles of diversions into the Moffat Water, Vasquez, Gumlick, and Harold D. Roberts Tunnels, the same water crossing the Continental Divide three times in the network of tunnels near Jones Pass.

Where does your water come from?

PAGE 50 Gazing across countless mountain summits on the Continental Divide from the summit of 13,294-foot James Peak on the last day of winter in 2011, I realized that this was all of the water we would have until the following spring. In this view, as snow on the right-hand (east) slope melts, it is "shed" to Denver and the South Platte River, and as snow on the left (west) side melts, it flows to the Fraser and Colorado Rivers. The spring of 2011 was wet and cold, and the mountains held snowpack well into summer, making it an outlier year in our twenty-three-year mega-drought in the Colorado River watershed.

TOP Getting an early morning start, Marla Ofstad studies a patch of alpine willow for sign of white-tailed ptarmigan, which are pure white in winter and can be nearly impossible to see when tucked under willow. This tundra and willow landscape just above timberline at around 11,500 feet provides excellent winter ptarmigan habitat in Colorado's Fraser River headwaters.

BOTTOM Fraser River water is diverted out of the Colorado River watershed through the Rocky Mountains in the Moffat Water Tunnel, where at the East Portal it joins South Boulder Creek on its way to Denver-area homes and lawns. Denver Water currently diverts about 60 percent of the Fraser's flow. About 80 percent of Colorado's freshwater originates on the Western Slope—the Colorado River side of the Rockies—while 80 percent of the population resides on the eastern half of the state in the Platte Basin watershed.

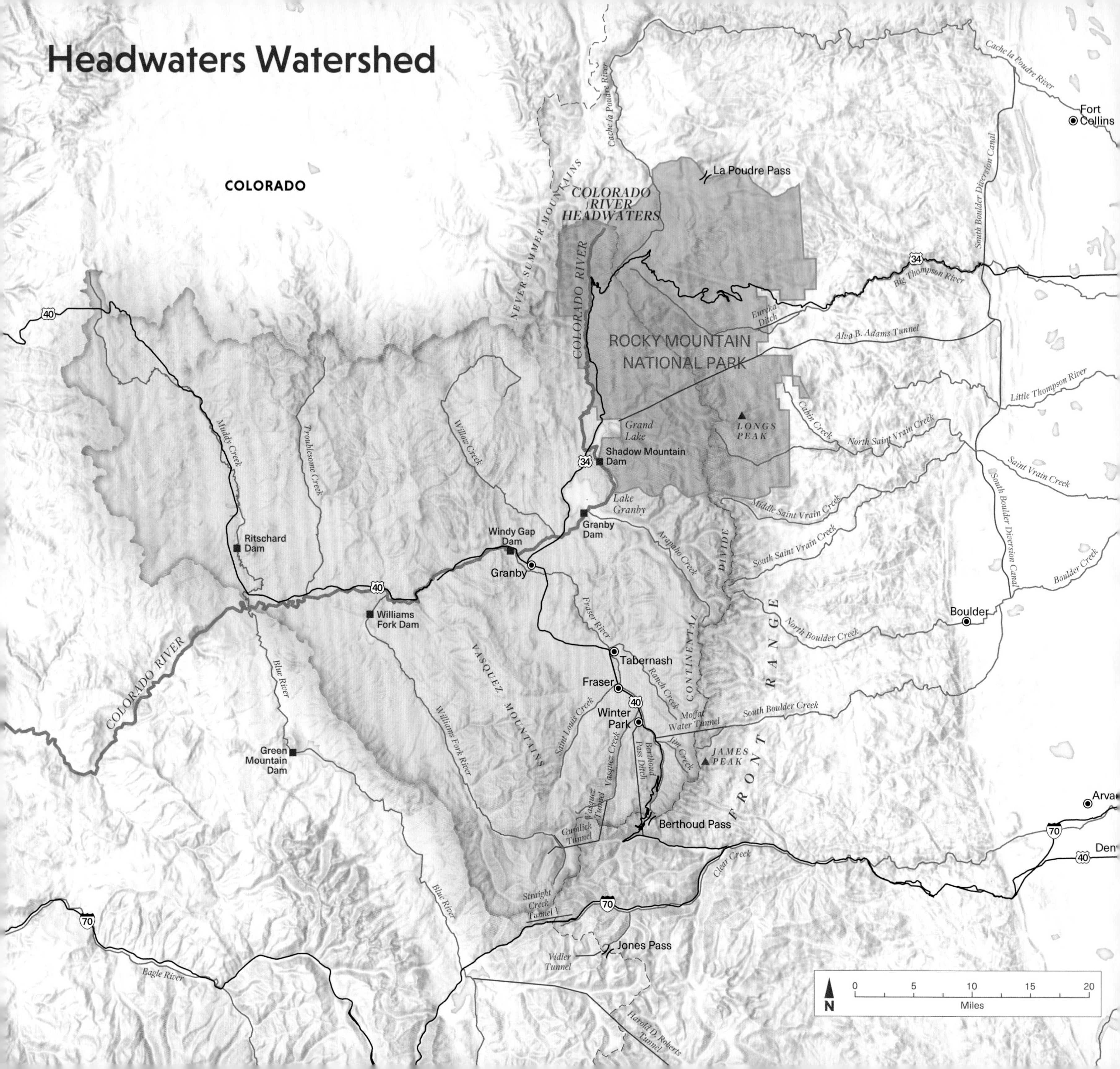
Headwaters Watershed
COLORADO
COLORADO RIVER HEADWATERS
NEVER SUMMER MOUNTAINS
Cache la Poudre River
La Poudre Pass
Fort Collins
South Boulder Diversion Canal
34
Big Thompson River
Eureka Ditch
Alva B. Adams Tunnel
ROCKY MOUNTAIN NATIONAL PARK
COLORADO RIVER
40
Muddy Creek
Troublesome Creek
Willow Creek
Grand Lake
LONGS PEAK
Cabin Creek
Little Thompson River
North Saint Vrain Creek
Shadow Mountain Dam
Saint Vrain Creek
Lake Granby
Middle Saint Vrain Creek
Granby Dam
Ritschard Dam
Windy Gap Dam
Granby
Arapaho Creek
DIVIDE
South Saint Vrain Creek
Boulder Creek
Williams Fork Dam
Fraser River
Boulder
North Boulder Creek
VASQUEZ MOUNTAINS
Tabernash
Fraser
Ranch Creek
CONTINENTAL
RANGE
Blue River
Winter Park
Saint Louis Creek
Moffat Water Tunnel
South Boulder Creek
Williams Fork River
Vasquez Creek
Berthoud Pass Ditch
Jim Creek
JAMES PEAK
FRONT
Green Mountain Dam
Vasquez Tunnel
Gumlick Tunnel
Berthoud Pass
Arvada
70
Denver
Clear Creek
Straight Creek Tunnel
Jones Pass
Vidler Tunnel
Eagle River
Harold D. Roberts Tunnel
0
5
10
15
20
Miles
N

Diverted Fraser River water bound for South Boulder Creek and Denver is pumped uphill through this pipeline east of the Winter Park Resort ski area.

Geographically, watershed boundaries are drawn by connecting all of the high points surrounding a river. The mountains *shed* snowmelt and rainfall, which flow into tributary rivulets, streams, creeks, and rivers, all easily diverted because water simply seeks to flow downstream. If you think of the main-stem river as a beating heart, tributaries are capillaries and arteries, adding life force to the river system.

What does it mean to say our water in Arvada comes from Rocky Mountain snowmelt or snowpack? My wife and I live in the South Platte River watershed, and for years I was certain that our home water source was James Peak, apex of the James Peak Wilderness and headwaters of South Boulder Creek. Yet I had no nuanced understanding of the history and mechanics of the plumbing system that reliably delivers clean drinking water to our tap. The Arvada city website lists South Boulder Creek, Clear Creek, and the Fraser River as our water sources, and all the water is impounded in Denver Water–owned Gross Reservoir, then Ralston Reservoir at the base of the foothills, before passing through a treatment facility for delivery throughout Arvada.

Imagine the Rocky Mountains deep into winter, holding a frozen reservoir of water in accumulated snow, its cornices drooping over steep mountain walls

LEFT Frost signals the end of the growing season for prairie smoke wildflowers along the Fraser River in the Colorado River headwaters.

OPPOSITE On a winter Friday night, Front Range skiers from the Denver metro area crest Berthoud Pass on US Highway 40 for the winding descent into the Fraser River valley and Winter Park Resort ski area. The Fraser valley is burgeoning with second homes, many owned by Front Range residents who straddle the Continental Divide by using Colorado River water on both sides of the Rockies.

like frozen waves waiting to release on the first warming days of spring. Clear Creek flow begins as a drop from snowpack atop 14,267-foot Torreys Peak, gathering snowmelt from the surrounding high peaks and building strength through the town of Idaho Springs, paralleling Interstate 70 as it falls from the mountains on its journey to Golden and the Denver metro area. Similarly, South Boulder Creek tumbles from James Peak to tiny high-alpine tarns and a necklace of alpine lakes along the eastern flanks of the Front Range, each lake outlet adding to the building current as it roars through spruce-fir forest until it reaches the East Portal of Moffat Water Tunnel, where the diverted Fraser River flow shoots from the tunnel to join South Boulder Creek. A transmountain diversion is a wholly unnatural aggression against a river, and here, 60 percent of the Fraser River's flow—water rights owned by Denver Water—has been diverted underneath the Continental Divide from the Colorado River watershed to the Platte Basin watershed to power metro Denver.

Berthoud Pass, at 11,307 feet, delineates the boundaries of the Colorado River and Platte Basin watersheds on Colorado's Front Range. From space, the Front Range mountains extend north from Berthoud Pass over James Peak and countless other high points, curving slightly northwest at 14,259-foot Longs Peak like a pointy index finger marking the true headwaters of the Colorado River in Rocky Mountain National Park's

Never Summer Range. The entire sea of mountain peaks and high valleys west of the Continental Divide, taking in the Fraser River and the west side of Rocky Mountain National Park, make up the headwaters region of the Colorado River.

First tributary of the Colorado River, the Fraser is thirty-two miles long, running from Berthoud Pass and James Peak, flowing past Winter Park Resort ski area and the Moffat Water Tunnel diversion, and receiving major tributaries Jim Creek, Vasquez Creek, Saint Louis Creek, and Ranch Creek before carving through Fraser Canyon to join the Colorado River at Windy Gap Reservoir, just west of Granby. In a sense, the Fraser River, heavily diverted to the big water users in the Denver metro area, with too many "straws" pulling flow from the river channel, is a smaller and emblematic vignette of threats caused by reduced flow throughout the Colorado River watershed. Our western rivers are stressed out, their snowpack diminished by climate change; river health is threatened by a constant state of tension between unnatural cycles of runoff and drawdown. And healthy rivers benefit every living thing.

The demands on the Fraser became clear to me when I first met Kirk Klancke, longtime conservationist and voice for the Fraser—a river keeper. He took me to the middle of a huge meadow in the center of the long, broad Fraser River valley and let me stand silently there for a bit before saying, "You probably wonder why I brought you here." Of course I wondered, since we had met to talk about the imperiled Fraser River, yet found ourselves on a parched meadow. Kirk told me to rotate around and study every crease in the Front Range and Vasquez Mountains, on up to the Never

KIRK KLANCKE

"If we fight over water,
we'll all come out losers."

TALL AND RANGY WITH AN EASY SMILE, Kirk Klancke settled in the Fraser River valley in 1971 for the "humanity" in the small, mostly logging town, beginning a love affair with the river and its people. He moved quickly from stonemason apprentice to small-business owner in his early twenties, skiing, fishing, and roaming the valley. In the early '70s, while exploring on Saint Louis Creek, Kirk came upon a large concrete diversion structure where the stream disappeared. That experience and a chance encounter with an "old-timer" who had concerns about reduced flow and river health—coupled with an undying love for the Fraser River—set Kirk on a course of community service, launching a half century of watershed conservation and rallying the headwaters community.

"There were no environmental regulations," Kirk says about the past, when in 1936 Fraser River waters were first diverted from the Rockies to Denver through the newly constructed Moffat Water Tunnel. In the 1970s, state water-quality regulations were weak; Denver Water, well within its water rights of 90 percent, was diverting just 60 percent of the Fraser to Denver, and no one was talking about stream health. The East Grand [County] Water Quality Board, with Kirk Klancke as president for fifteen years, began monitoring streams; its current mission is to monitor the headwaters of the Colorado River in the Fraser River watershed. Conversations with

Kirk Klancke in his classic '54 Chevy pickup truck near his Fraser River valley home

Denver Water followed, which in time evolved into seeking collaborative solutions. Indeed, Kirk is fond of saying, "Engineered problems need engineered solutions."

On a cool, cloudy October morning, I joined Kirk, who also is president of the Trout Unlimited (TU) Headwaters Chapter, and a group gathered near the town of Tabernash, everyone layering up and donning waders for the unsettled autumn day. Here on Fraser Flats, site of a major Grand County Learning by Doing Cooperative Effort stream-renovation project, a pile of shocking poles, nets, buckets, and other gear was laid out riverside. Jon Ewert, a Colorado Parks and Wildlife biologist, gave instructions on how to move through the river channel in line and net stunned fish to study fish biomass, recording fish density, size, and new native hatch on Fraser Flats. The shocking poles jolted fish with an electric current, temporarily stunning them long enough to be handled and released unharmed. This collaborative conservation study brought together Denver Water employees, TU volunteers, Colorado Parks and Wildlife, and high school students, standing knee-deep side by side for river conservation. The event was

LEFT Colorado Parks and Wildlife biologist Jon Ewert, holding a brown trout on Fraser Flats in an October biomass study, says, "We're learning a lot about the most effective approaches to the design of physical stream restoration projects, and we take what we learn from each one and incorporate it into the design of the next one, so that each project turns out better and more effective than the last."

OPPOSITE Trout Unlimited, Denver Water, Colorado Parks and Wildlife, volunteers, and hardy high school students gather on Fraser Flats for an October biomass study, part of the Grand County Learning by Doing Cooperative Effort for the health of the Fraser River in the Colorado River headwaters. Fish are temporarily shocked, their species, size, and weight are recorded, then they are released unharmed.

possible because of a conversation Kirk and others had started with Denver Water decades ago.

Upstream of Winter Park Resort, a partnership including TU Headwaters Chapter, Denver Water, Colorado Department of Transportation, and East Grand Water Quality Board addressed the problem of accumulated road sand and salt sediment laid down on the highway for safe winter driving. For years, Kirk had lobbied for an "engineered solution," and eventually a settling pond was built to catch sand and salt sediment that would otherwise get washed into the river and flushed downstream. The road sediment no longer fills voids in river cobble where aquatic insects and sculpin thrive, the foundations of a healthy river system.

Conservation requires nurturing, and thanks in large part to Kirk's leadership over decades, the Colorado's headwaters community is widely engaged in Fraser River conservation as the relationship with Denver Water has evolved into a partnership. Fly fishers carrying thermometers to check stream temperatures became a community science study, leading to data collection protocol, sowing the seeds of the Learning by Doing restoration on Fraser Flats, a success by any measure. At Fraser Flats back on that cool October morning, the day's biomass study revealed a healthy sculpin population and trout minnows, wild hatched in the river—hopeful signs of recovery in a restored river reach. ✲

Summer Range at the very headwaters of the mighty Colorado. As we stood there on crunchy, dry, midsummer grass, Kirk explained that every single creek flowing from the high mountain peaks has a diversion structure on it, and every drop is spoken for—every drop in the entire watershed of the Colorado. Once that settled in, I began to see this ribbon of blue mountain river in a different light: engineered and owned.

On any Friday night, as Denver and Front Range travelers merge with tourists from everywhere, headed for a weekend of adventure in the mountains, a steady stream of cars flowing west drops in over Berthoud Pass to the Fraser River valley. In a little more than an hour's drive from the Denver metro area, motorists are transported over the Continental Divide into the Colorado River headwaters region, past Winter Park Resort ski area and the Moffat Water Tunnel's West Portal, into the charming mountain towns of Winter Park and Fraser. More than a million visitors, many from the Denver metro area, descend on the Fraser River valley annually, seeking deep powder turns, world-class hiking and mountain biking, and a chance to land a muscular Fraser River trout. Back in the 1950s, these waters were President Dwight D. Eisenhower's favorite place to fish, and they are now graced by his statue on the river in Fraser. Stories still circulate of the leader of the free world sneaking away from his Secret Service detail to wet a line.

All those visitors from the Denver area use Colorado River water both at home and away, on both sides of the Rockies, metaphorically straddling the Continental Divide. Downstream from her headwaters, the Colorado continues more than 1,400 miles, receiving major tributaries—the Blue, Eagle, Gunnison, and Dolores Rivers—adding flow on her way to confluence with the Green River in Utah's Canyonlands National Park. At scale, residents of Salt Lake City, Denver, Albuquerque, Las Vegas, Phoenix, Tucson, San Diego, and Los Angeles, all built on diverted transmountain Colorado River water, owe their existence to the Colorado River—they, too, metaphorically straddle the Continental Divide.

ACROSS THE DEEP FRASER VALLEY FROM James Peak and a few switchbacks below Berthoud Pass, Second Creek flows from accumulated snowpack draining from the high points of a giant U-shaped alpine cirque, dropping more than 2,000 feet to the Fraser River at valley bottom. The hiking trail to Broome Hut, in the Tenth Mountain Division hut system, ascends quickly through mixed spruce-fir forest, much of it standing beetle kill, to a high-point reveal of the alpine bowl and Broome Hut, just below timberline. Sometimes near the hut I hear white-tailed ptarmigan calling, described by renowned author and bird illustrator David Allen Sibley in *Sibley Birds West* as a "rapid clucking *pik pik pik pik piKEEA*." The high-pitched call is often the only way to locate these camouflage specialists in big, open country. Beyond the hut and through a patch of dense conifer forest that marks the line where tall trees end, sparse, stunted, gnarled krummholz trees dot patches of alpine willow, the lovely alpine creek winding through it all.

The personality of this place shifts dramatically through the seasons as summer's tie-dyed wildflower meadow and alpine tundra are buried under a blanket of white, Second Creek gurgling beneath snow and ice. This classic Colorado Rockies basin is a stronghold for

TOP Sunrise lights the Vasquez Mountains over the Winter Park Resort ski area, holding a skiff of October snow. At the base of the ski area, the twin bores of the Moffat Water Tunnel move Front Range tourists and skiers by train through one tunnel and ferry 60 percent of the Fraser River through the water tunnel in a major transmountain diversion to the Denver metro area. (LightHawk aerial support)

BOTTOM The Fraser River, the Colorado's first tributary, has been dredged, with restoration ongoing through Fraser Flats south of Rocky Mountain National Park, Colorado, to keep the river cooler for trout, with defined banks, point bars, riffles, and replanted willow—vegetation for birds and shade for trout. Reworking the channel is a project of the Grand County Learning by Doing Cooperative Effort to support stream health in the Colorado's headwaters region.

White-tailed ptarmigan are adapted to life in the harsh Rocky Mountain alpine zone and the Colorado River headwaters, spending their entire life cycle above timberline. Ptarmigan thrive, and actually gain weight, in winter by burying themselves in snow for insulation when at rest, with tiny alpine willow buds the size of a chia seed making up about 90 percent of their winter diet. These camouflage experts will change to the mottled colors of talus rock through summer breeding season.

the white-tailed ptarmigan, North America's smallest grouse species, which uses camouflage as a primary defense strategy by transitioning seasonally: in winter to pure white (except for black eyes and beak) and through summer breeding season to mottled browns and grays, perfectly matching talus rock. Remarkably, white-tailed ptarmigan spend their entire life cycle on alpine tundra above timberline.

Marla and I have adopted this basin as a place to return to through the seasons, as wandering glorious alpine tundra while searching for ptarmigan becomes the most enjoyable of outings. This high mountain wonderland demands that we linger to study the nuances and subtle changes of season, to know its rhythms and characters. So we wake in what feels like the middle of the night to drive up I-70, reaching the trailhead in darkness to witness the miracle of sunrise from a high mountain ridge enveloped in primal wildness. Each time feels both familiar and new, fresh and exhilarating.

In winter white, ptarmigan rely on alpine willow habitat, where tiny willow buds the size of chia seeds make up 90 percent of their winter diet. As snowstorms blanket the landscape, just the tops of willow are visible, with three-toed ptarmigan tracks leaving clues where the birds are feeding. Like tiny snowshoes, ptarmigan feet are covered in feathers for buoyancy in deep snow, part of their remarkable adaptation to the high alpine. Studying this world of blue and white reveals more tracks: impressions of wing tips with a softball-size round center show where the birds have slept—white-tailed ptarmigan bury themselves up to a foot deep to insulate themselves from subzero conditions. These remarkable birds thrive, and even gain weight, through winter, conserving energy in lengthy sedentary periods, then pecking voraciously at willow buds, their whole life cycle choreographed to the arrival and departure of snowpack and life above timberline.

I imagine the life stirring beneath the snowpack, where diminutive American pika feed on a hay pile of grasses and wildflowers gathered over the summer. Pika, cutest fur balls in the rabbit family, are tucked among talus rocks around the edges of the cirque, using mountain snowpack for insulation. Pika don't hibernate, instead lowering their metabolism and body temperature to conserve energy. Meanwhile, hibernating yellow-bellied marmots huddle together in hay-lined burrow rooms beneath the snowpack, living on fat stored in autumn, their body temperature dropping to 41 degrees Fahrenheit, their active heart rate reducing from 180–200 beats per minute to just 30, and taking just one or two breaths each minute, for two-hundred-plus days of hibernation.

Leaping between rocks, an American pika carries flowers and grasses to a hay pile tucked in a talus field at around 12,000 feet elevation in Rocky Mountain National Park, Colorado. Pika dry and cure their larder of grasses, sedges, forbs, lichens, and thistle for storage in their winter den, sustenance beneath the mountain snowpack through winter.

NEXT PAGES Sunrise paints the banks of Ranch Creek in autumnal reds as dramatic clouds hang over James Peak and the Fraser River headwaters in Colorado.

Snowpack is both frozen river and seasonal reservoir, patiently waiting to release life-giving power come spring; for where there is water, there is life—even in frozen water. These animals, the alpine willow, grasses, wildflowers, and forest rely on snowpack for survival just as we do, no separation.

AS THE FRASER RIVER FLOWS DOWNSTREAM from Berthoud Pass and the surrounding peaks, past the Winter Park Resort ski area and the towns of Winter Park and Fraser, the river course levels out, meandering through a popular trout-fishing reach called Fraser Flats. After runoff from snowpack peaks in early to mid-June and Denver Water diverts its share, the Fraser's flow is greatly reduced. Here, at Fraser Flats, the river is exposed to blazing summer sun; once heavily grazed by cattle, the flats lacked the woody vegetation needed to stabilize banks and cool the waters with afternoon shade. Trout need cold water and become heat stressed when stream temperatures reach 65 degrees Fahrenheit, as dissolved oxygen escapes into the atmosphere, and they can die when the stream reaches 74 degrees. The Trout Unlimited (TU) Headwaters Chapter, a nonprofit dedicated to protecting and restoring rivers, such as the cold-water fisheries in the headwaters, recommends that anglers carry a thermometer in their pack to measure stream temperatures or, absent a thermometer, simply stop fishing at 1:00 p.m. to minimize stressing fish and unintended fish kills.

Fond of saying "Conservation begins with a conversation," Kirk Klancke, working with TU and Grand County, started a conversation with Denver Water that led to the Grand County Learning by Doing Cooperative Effort project on Fraser Flats, which seeks "to maintain and, where reasonably possible, restore or enhance the aquatic environment in the Fraser, Williams Fork, and Colorado River basins and their tributaries in Grand County, Colorado." Thanks to this major stream renovation, Fraser Flats now holds good cold-water habitat for trout and woody vegetation for birds. In June, yellow warblers sing sweetly from the tops of restored willow, protecting nesting territories, while broad-tailed hummingbirds feed on willow blooms. Savannah sparrows add a high-pitched buzzing rhythm to the soundscape. An October 2018 biomass study on the Fraser Flats reach revealed a natural hatch of brown trout fingerlings and a healthy sculpin population, signaling the beginnings of recovery on this mile-long stretch of river. Dedicated volunteers continue planting new willow stakes, monitoring stream health, and educating anglers about ethical use of the resource.

On my first tour of the Fraser River valley with Kirk, there was heavy equipment in the stream channel, setting point bars to direct flow, stabilizing banks, increasing stream depth and velocity. One hundred fifty volunteers came to the Fraser to harvest and plant 4,600 willow stakes and 90 cottonwoods, restoring woody vegetation for the health of the river. With $200,000 raised, what began with fishermen carrying thermometers and gathering data became a major collaboration, led by TU, with Devil's Thumb Ranch, Denver Water, Northern Water, Grand County, and Colorado Parks and Wildlife, for this biologically significant reach on the Fraser—the first significant tributary of the Colorado.

On the Platte Basin side of the Rockies, another collaborative effort is being made to address water issues, as Denver Water proceeds with a contentious

A female broad-tailed hummingbird feeds on a May willow bloom along Colorado's Fraser River.

planned expansion of Gross Reservoir, raising the height of the dam where diverted Fraser River water is stored for Denver and the Front Range. Although adding capacity to a dam in the South Platte watershed sounds counterintuitive in a time of water shortage for the Colorado watershed, Denver Water and TU Headwaters Chapter believe the additional capacity will yield more flexibility for releasing water back into the Fraser when and where it's needed.

Eighty percent of Colorado's freshwater originates on the Western Slope and 80 percent of the population lives on the Front Range, exemplifying the long-standing tension between big-city demands and the more rural western half of the state. Denver Water currently diverts 60 percent of the Fraser River through the Moffat Water Tunnel, and it has committed to being a responsible steward in both the Colorado River and Platte Basin watersheds. In the early summer heat of 2021, snow runoff peaked early, on June 3, and Fraser Flats heated up as a paltry snowpack melted off the high peaks while Denver Water diverted flow to meet demand. With the Fraser drawn down to just fifty cubic feet per second during peak runoff from mid-May to mid-June, Kirk Klancke, Trout Unlimited, and other Western Slope partners asked Denver Water to release more water into the Fraser to prevent a fish kill. Denver Water responded, voluntarily releasing about 11,000 acre-feet of water into the Fraser River and major tributary stream Ranch Creek to cool the river and improve habitat for aquatic insects and fish. Conservation that began with a conversation decades ago kept the river a little cooler and helped prevent a fish die-off through a blazing summer.

Here in the Colorado's headwaters, where rivers are born, where dynamic forces of mountains make their own weather—seasons of monsoon, snow, and wildfire—where the pulse of human and wild communities is tethered to healthy headwaters rivers, we can continue hoping for big winters to quell our water security worries. But climate models predict less snow in the coming decades, telling us we'll have to listen to the land and the river we have, that we'll need to conserve, listen to one another, and work in community. Collaborating to save the Fraser, integral to headwaters health, is one of these stories of saving the Colorado.

High in the Rocky Mountain National Park headwaters, the Colorado River burbles under ice and between mounds of snow at the peak of winter.

TOP Burned ridges of the Never Summer Range contrast with an unburned patch of forest in this aerial view. Only 10 percent of the land within the fire boundary was unburned, and 53 percent of sampled soil ranged from moderately to severely burned, an important predictor of erosion and water-quality impacts. (LightHawk aerial support)

BOTTOM LEFT The autumn 2020 East Troublesome fire behaved like a firestorm, bending mature trees into arches and burning entire mountainsides. (LightHawk aerial support)

BOTTOM RIGHT Thick smoke from the Williams Fork fire filled the Colorado River headwaters in August 2020, with Longs Peak just visible on the (upper left) horizon, in a wildfire season that lasted deep into autumn. Rocky Mountain winters now arrive about three weeks later in autumn and end about three weeks earlier in spring than historical averages.

TOP Native monument plants emerge from blackened, encrusted soil in Colorado's Rocky Mountain National Park, beginning the process of renewal in the East Troublesome fire's burn scar.

BOTTOM The Colorado River winds from Rocky Mountain National Park into Sun Valley Guest Ranch, leveled on October 22, 2020, when the East Troublesome fire exploded on winds in excess of 100 miles per hour, burning more than 125,000 acres in a single day. The fire breached the Continental Divide and nearly merged with the Cameron fire—the two largest wildfires in Colorado history raged well into autumn when we expect "termination dust," the first snowfalls of the season that signal a transition to winter. (LightHawk aerial support)

Chapter 2

SEEDSKADEE AND THE GREEN RIVER

River of the Sage-Grouse

SEARCHING, I LOCATED A FAINT TRAIL heading toward the Green River through waist-high sagebrush, until a left turn on a mule deer trail pointed to the 300-foot-tall broad tawny bluff that seems to rise from the river. Between river and bluff, I tunneled through thick vegetation to find a thin passage against a cool wall with swallow nests above, looking like primitive jugs plastered at a forty-five-degree angle beneath the overhang. The crux of this exploration was a boot-width section where gripping a tree belay kept one foot dry, the river current swift against the cut bank. Walking became easier before I found my way around a wetland where I startled a northern harrier, flushed from her nest in a forest of tall cattails and sedges. I moved on swiftly without peeking so she could tend to her nest.

The air was humid and still that June morning, with a pleasant riparian mustiness, as I found my way to the base of the tall bluff where a bobcat had been spotted the afternoon before. A prairie falcon screeched loudly from the top of the bluff, and I suspected there was a nest nearby. Swallows swirled above, gorging on

Sunset lingers on Stroud and Sulphur Peaks where the headwaters of the Green River plunge from Peak Lake and the Wind River Range in the Bridger–Teton Wilderness, Wyoming.

PAGE 72 On a scrape above the Green River, an adult prairie falcon feeds chipmunk to hungry chicks. Observing the family over a week revealed that their diet also included Wyoming ground squirrel, both prey items captured in the sagebrush lands bordering the Green River in southwest Wyoming.

mosquitoes and darting into nests just overhead. The bluff had looked like solid blocks of sandstone from across the river—close up, it was mudstone conglomerate studded with rounded cobble, the vertical wall of the bluff creased and eroded by rain runoff and time, then baked stiff and crunchy in the summer heat. I picked my way up a small ravine to find another route to the river bluff rim in my hunt for sign of the bobcat: it had been perfectly framed on the edge of a riverside cave in an image captured on an angler's cell phone. From the top of the bluff, I watched the river flowing past a boat launch where fishermen were readying a drift boat for a day on world-class trout waters; a small band of mule deer browsed in cottonwood and willow across the river as pelicans coasted the river's edge around a big right-hand bend before disappearing from sight. A bald eagle raced across the face of the bluff intently looking for an easy meal, his gold eye flashing by in an instant.

BORN IN THE WIND RIVER RANGE, THE GREEN River is the biggest tributary—in length and volume—of the Colorado, winding 730 miles south from western Wyoming through eastern Utah to reach its confluence with the Colorado in Canyonlands National Park. Thirty-six miles of the Green River flows through Seedskadee National Wildlife Refuge (NWR) and the sageland steppe and semidesert uplands of the Little Colorado Desert in southwest Wyoming. The name Seedskadee is a mountain-man derivation

TOP A small herd of pronghorn race across snow-covered sagebrush flats in Seedskadee National Wildlife Refuge, Wyoming. Pronghorn, the western hemisphere's fastest land mammal, are neither goat nor antelope but a singular twenty-million-year-old species.

BOTTOM The only inscription by legendary mountain man, trapper, army scout, and wilderness guide James (Jim) Bridger is carved into limestone at Names Hill, where emigrants and Indigenous people left their mark on the old Oregon Trail at the Green River crossing and rendezvous site, upstream from Seedskadee National Wildlife Refuge.

from the Shoshone word *sisk-a-dee-agie*, meaning "river of the sage grouse." Imperiled greater sage-grouse still walk broods of flightless, half-grown chicks across sagebrush uplands to the refuge in early summer, where they feed on insects, seeds, and leafy vegetation along the river. Indigenous peoples have used this landscape since Pleistocene ice sheets receded. Nomadic Shoshone people fanned across Seedskadee seven hundred years ago to hunt the Green River Basin's wildlife bounty of bison, pronghorn, bighorn sheep, mule deer, elk, and sage-grouse. Seedskadee and the meandering Green River sustained Indigenous people until the arrival of Euro-Americans brought rapid change. In 1824 fur trappers Thomas Fitzpatrick, Jim Bridger, Jedediah Smith, and Etienne Provost discovered the South Pass on the north end of the Red Desert, following Shoshone trails on their

descent to the confluence where the Green River absorbs the Big Sandy River in what is now the Seedskadee National Wildlife Refuge.

The Green River crossing at the Big Sandy confluence, now within the refuge, saw a progression of human migrations across the Green for decades. The ferries were run first by mountain men from 1843 to

1850, then by Mormons led by Brigham Young until 1858. Hundreds of thousands of emigrants crossed this humble stretch of the Green by ferry while seeking fortune in the opening of the American West. Collectively, around 350,000 people emigrated west on the California, Oregon, and Mormon Trails from 1843 to 1869, with as many as fifty ferries operating in a fifty-mile stretch of the Green River. Roughly 10 percent of emigrants perished on the perilous two-thousand-mile journey. At Names Hill, upstream from Seedskadee, Native American pictographs and carved names near the California and Oregon Trails crossing are a living record of westward expansion before rail. When emigrants crossed the Green, they had just traveled a forty-mile waterless section across the sagebrush lands of the Little Colorado Desert.

Log homesteader cabins dating to the late 1800s dot Seedskadee, offering a glimpse into early settlement, sheepherding, and cattle ranching in this arid country with the Green River running through it. Two identical concrete houses on opposite sides of the river that appear oddly out of place in the riverine landscape hold a macabre history. In 1916 Ed Karel and his wife homesteaded here, and across the river Ed's half brother, Joe, built in sight of his brother a small concrete house, which he shared with an elderly man named Mr. Shaw. The brothers got into a drunken argument while both Mr. Shaw and Mrs. Karel were away, with Ed suspicious of an affair between Joe and his wife. The brothers shot each other and were discovered by Mr. Shaw a few days later, magpies picking at the bloated corpses.

Private cattle ranches dotted the landscape around the current Fontenelle Dam and Seedskadee NWR until Fontenelle and Flaming Gorge Dams were planned. The Colorado River Storage Project Act of 1956 authorized the US Bureau of Reclamation to acquire lands to offset critical wildlife habitat that would be flooded by impoundments behind the Fontenelle and Flaming Gorge Dams. Constructed from 1961 to 1964, the Fontenelle Dam on the Green River is the northernmost dam in the Colorado River Storage Project. Fontenelle Dam and Reservoir were built primarily to irrigate farmlands in the surrounding unplowed dry sagelands. In 1962 an experimental hay farm under the Seedskadee Project was irrigated with Green River water pumped uphill by generators, but after ten years it failed because the high, arid valley freezes every month of the year, which is simply too cold for producing hay. The hay farm, now covered in nonnative grass, remains as evidence of folly in the dam-building era.

Just below the dam, the Bureau of Reclamation in 1965 created Seedskadee National Wildlife Refuge by purchasing private land. The Green River meanders through Seedskadee NWR for thirty-six river miles, refuge for more than two hundred species, its 26,400 acres managed by the US Fish and Wildlife Service.

Downstream from the refuge, the Green River flows past immense mines excavated to extract trona, a powdery white mineral that is the primary source of sodium carbonate in the United States, which is used in toothpaste, baking soda, laundry detergents, and glass, among a host of uses. The river continues south through the namesake town of Green River, Wyoming (there is also a town of Green River, Utah), launching point in 1869 for John Wesley Powell's famous first-ever Colorado River exploration; the town is about

A trio of river otters haul up on Green River shore ice with a fresh catch of an endemic American whitefish. Wyoming's Seedskadee National Wildlife Refuge has a healthy otter population estimated at more than thirty pairs of breeding adults, an indicator of good water quality and abundant fish stocks. Seedskadee river otters generally prey on crayfish and slower-moving fish like native white sucker—scat sampling at hollowed-log den sites has revealed a strong preference for crayfish.

thirty-five miles south of Seedskadee and just north of Flaming Gorge Reservoir, dedicated by former first lady Lady Bird Johnson in 1964. The Green winds south through the Flaming Gorge Reservoir and Dam and is joined downstream by the Yampa, Duchesne, White, Price, and San Rafael Rivers; its confluence with the Colorado deep in Canyonlands National Park is a meeting of calm, sediment-laden waters that belies the roiling rapids of Cataract Canyon just downstream. Beginning as a river of ice, the Green River has traveled 730 miles when its flow joins the Colorado River in the Colorado Plateau.

RIVER PHOTOGRAPHY IS OFTEN ABOUT PICKing a spot and hunkering down, camouflaged, patient, and ready. On my first trip to Seedskadee, I texted friend and colleague Mike Forsberg, frustrated by the unreal numbers of wildlife opportunities and my inability to make decent images as I raced from one spot to another. Mike's response: "Go to the river and just breathe." Refuge manager Tom Koerner coached me similarly, so after a few expeditions I'd grown accustomed to tucking into a bank camo'd up and watching the river flow—going to the river to just breathe.

The open waters on the Green through Seedskadee don't freeze here, due to swift flow from the Fontenelle Dam upstream. On the coldest mornings, ice floes scrape along shore ice and bond together in flowing slush as ice fog grips the channel. There is no "w" on these mornings—locals prefer not to say "wind" for fear of inviting Wyoming's renowned gusts—just pure blue, unshakable cold. My truck thermometer read minus 27 degrees Fahrenheit when I set out on one of

OPPOSITE Volunteer Russ Barnes trims willow stakes for replanting and restoration along the shores of the Green River in Seedskadee National Wildlife Refuge.

RIGHT Protecting nesting territory in early June, a marsh wren takes flight to land on a cattail and sing his sweet song, making several stops on a continuous circuit in his riparian habitat. As spring warms to summer, the frenetic activity of seemingly every living thing in the wetland is both beautifully choreographed and chaotic.

those mornings, headed for a bend in the river where an island creates a side channel, slowing current on the outside bend along the island.

Trumpeter swans, North America's largest waterfowl species, like to roost on a slab of shore ice on outside river bends. It's common to see swans in flight over the cottonwood forest across the river and cruising the placid waters in family groups along the island's shore. At dawn, bald eagles will leave their downstream roost, tracing cottonwood tops to reach a fishing spot on a tall tree somewhere upstream. While I thought about my chilled toes—a lot—the high-pitched chirps of a bald eagle pierced fog as ice formed and flowed past, scraping and building shore ice. Goldeneye ducks floated around the river bend, diving between ice chunks for crayfish. After drifting past the bend, they'd fly low upstream, wings whistling, landing back where they started, riding a conveyor belt on another icy crayfish float. No swans appeared in the fog. Cold seeped deeper into my core as I waited.

Suddenly there was a movement—something dark, maybe fifty yards out on the point of the island. As I squinted to focus, a river otter appeared from an ice hole next to an otter slide on the edge of the bank.

On winter evenings at Seedskadee National Wildlife Refuge, trumpeter swans fly over the Green River channel in waves, dropping into still waters or onto shore-ice evening roosts. North America's largest waterfowl species needs open water to feed on aquatic vegetation, with a strong preference for sago pondweed, and much of the Green River in Seedskadee remains open and ice-free with Fontenelle Reservoir just upstream. The swan on the right is collared—trumpeter swans have been documented migrating as far as the Grand Canyon and back, connecting most of the Colorado River watershed in flight.

Then there were two otters, rolling in a playful ball for a moment, popping in and out of the small opening. When one, then the other, disappeared, I thought they were gone—until an otter emerged from a bank hole across the channel next to a huge beaver lodge. In just those few moments, the otters told me a lot about their home. Revisiting the site, I witnessed otters swimming back and forth across the channel and traced their shadows and movement echoing just beneath the ice.

WILDLIFE LIKE THOSE OTTERS DON'T NECESsarily need pristine nature; they need cold, clear water and a human understanding of the habitat needs of nature, the elements and drivers of a functioning river system. Seedskadee's wild heart is woody riparian vegetation and river as refuge flowing through the Little Colorado Desert. The refuge is a dynamic laboratory for studying habitat treatments and how wildlife respond.

We know, for instance, that the imperiled cottonwood-willow ecosystem stabilizes stream banks and provides food and shelter for everything that floats, flies, or browses—that moose, flycatchers, and warblers really like willow. Until 1964, with the construction of the Fontenelle Dam, the Green River could flood in spring and sprawl across open floodplains, nurturing new willow and cottonwood, the floodwaters and woody vegetation in a symbiotic relationship at exactly the right seasonal moment. With river flow tightly controlled by dams, western rivers no longer flood during spring runoff. Cottonwoods live out their life cycles of a century or more and die off, and willows gradually recede or get consumed by browsing cattle and wildlife.

A century of grazing had left Seedskadee refuge lands on both sides of the Green River wanting for willow and new cottonwood recruitment. Willow restoration is painstakingly done by hand, much of it by volunteers and the Youth Conservation Corps, a federal summer youth-employment program for environmental stewardship and responsibility. Willow stakes are clipped to be planted in wet riparian soil, each willow stake a hopeful gesture for songbird, moose, and porcupine. New cottonwood saplings are staked and wrapped in fencing to protect the thin trees from browsing by moose and deer. Raising a tree to live a hundred years takes patience, time, and water. Where cottonwood, willow, and river current converge, moose, bald eagles, and songbirds are here in big numbers. About a dozen trumpeter swan pairs stay on the refuge through breeding season, nesting in wetlands fed by old irrigation ditches. Seedskadee is still a working landscape where habitat needs are clearly being met and wildlife are responding, finding refuge.

Greater sage-grouse gather on the rim of the Green River before taking a short flight across the river to feed on insects and forbs in a wet meadow. The name Seedskadee is a mountain-man derivation of *sisk-a-dee-agie*, a Shoshone word meaning "river of the sage grouse." Sage-grouse hens bring their broods to the refuge in early June, where they feed along the river before fledging and returning to the surrounding sagelands of the Little Colorado Desert.

An adult bobcat pauses on a bluff above the Green River at sunset in Seedskadee National Wildlife Refuge, Wyoming.

The namesake greater sage-grouse arrive in June, when females walk still-flightless fledglings across open sagelands to raise them along the river. The chicks are pretty big by the time they get to Seedskadee, big enough for the hike through a sea of sagebrush. There are known leks (mating grounds) in the sagelands around Seedskadee, yet no one knows exactly where so many grouse hens with broods come from. But they do show up, roosting in the sage and walking to the river in the mornings. They go to the river to eat forbs and insects while the young grouse develop to digest a diet of mostly sagebrush leaves.

On summer evenings, it's common to see a sage hen with two or three trailing chicks walking up from the river and crossing the main road before they disappear into the sage for the evening. On three straight summer mornings, I witnessed a group of sage-grouse gather on the high bank above the river, then fly across to feed in a wet meadow beneath a bald eagle nest. Surely the sage-grouse were aware of the active eagle nest, and I wondered about their habitat choice, but then considered that the two species have evolved together over millennia.

MY EXPLORATORY JUNE BOBCAT SEARCH revealed an alternate way to the river where I could make a steep descent from the top of the bluff, rather than traversing the sketchy game trail along its base. For a week, I hiked up and down the bluff on vertical terrain with the aid of cobble-studded mudstone for traction. Several times I was accompanied by a goofy-looking domestic sheep ram, left behind when the sage was temporarily grazed by sheep in midsummer. The rotund ram would appear out of nowhere and lead me to the edge, then look at me with a peculiar side-eye before heading down. He'd then wait on a flat spot halfway before leading me to the river, and I'd thank him in a quiet voice, grateful for the amusement. He'd be gone as swiftly as he arrived, a fuzzy white ghost.

Sometimes, while I walked at river's edge with swallows circling, an otter would poke its head out in the middle of the river to study me for a moment before vanishing in the current. Prairie falcons screeched their heads off when I walked beneath a section at the base of the bluff, their nest on a flat scrape overhead. I waited with a long lens each day, knowing food deliveries were coming when the three chicks made their high-pitched calls, mouths gaping, the racket bouncing off stone walls. The deliveries alternated between chipmunk and ground squirrel, the adults tearing off little pieces to place in waiting mouths. The prey animal disappeared in five or ten minutes, and usually one adult

A bobcat kitten confidently negotiates the edge of a bluff above the Green River in the Wyoming dusk.

would remain on the crest of the bluff as lookout, the pair talking back and forth.

Running out of time on my next-to-last night at Seedskadee, I sat on my bumper with a cold beverage thinking about bobcats and the incredible witnessing of wildlife I'd experienced in the refuge over the previous week. I knew that spotting the bobcat was a needle-in-a-haystack situation and decided it was okay if I didn't see it, that it's about the journey or something like that. Just then, a brownish flash dove into a narrow crease maybe thirty yards distant. A quick calculation pointed me to another cut in the bluff that might parallel where the animal—which I believed was a bobcat—had gone.

Dropping down into a shallow gap on the rim and setting up behind a sagebrush, I waited while studying the steep mudstone wall with a small cave opening. The bobcat mom emerged on the canyon wall, then rested on a tiny ledge, a pair of kittens walking confidently along the rim above her. I held my breath as one of the kittens descended about twenty feet to reach mom just below the little cave. There, in fading light, on the slope of a bluff over the Green River, the kitten nursed. It turned out there were three kittens; maybe the little cave, where one of the kittens stood in the opening, was the natal cave.

I went back one more night and waited, camouflaged in a gillie suit in hopes of seeing the little family one more time. Just as the sun dropped behind the distant Wyoming Range, a bobcat appeared on the ridge, noble against the muted pastel sunset. She moved a few feet and gazed soulfully into dusk, then moved on. A river gift.

TOM KOERNER

"Managing for wildlife doesn't mean put a sign up or a fence up—it means you have to simulate historical ecological processes . . . and you have to be able to explain it, because we work for the public."

AT EACH STOP IN A LENGTHY CAREER in conservation management, Nebraska native and Seedskadee National Wildlife Refuge manager Tom Koerner has sought "ecosystem drivers" to identify and replicate natural processes that enable nature to rebound. Inspired by Aldo Leopold and early pioneers of conservation, Tom has used controlled burns and controlled cattle grazing to mimic vegetation disturbance where bison once roamed and help restore wetlands in Nebraska's Rainwater Basin NWR and LeCreek NWR. Waterfowl returned quickly—a win for watershed health. But Seedskadee, with a dam just upstream on the Green River and a history of heavy grazing in the Little Colorado Desert, presents a range of challenges.

Cottonwood gallery forest and willow are essential to riparian ecosystem health by providing woody habitat and food for wildlife, shade, and bank stabilization, but neither tree species was doing well at Seedskadee when Tom arrived a decade ago. Studying the coyote willow, Tom saw tiny stems sticking up with roots beneath, but as soon as the willow "poked its head up" it was getting bitten off and trampled on the edge of cut banks. Browsed by moose, porcupine, deer, and cattle, willow had reached a tipping point. A "let it grow" strategy that keeps cattle out allows the undisturbed willow to respond, putting up leaves, storing energy in roots, and growing above browsing height in three to five years. Today, flourishing coyote willow benefits beaver, moose, and birds. The refuge remains a good neighbor—cattle and seasonal sheep use water-access lanes called water gaps that end in U-shaped

OPPOSITE Refuge manager Tom Koerner above the horseshoe bend in the Green River at sunset in Seedskadee National Wildlife Refuge, Wyoming

TOP Someone has to take the leap. American pelicans roam the Green River channels throughout Seedskadee in summer, finding healthy fish populations to scoop in their massive bills. Thick bodied, with a nine-foot wingspan, the American pelican is one of North America's largest waterbirds.

BOTTOM In autumn, kokanee salmon swim upstream from Flaming Gorge Reservoir to spawn in Seedskadee waters. Kokanee are commonly called a landlocked sockeye salmon, and although nonnative, these humpbacked bright-red fish contribute mightily to biomass in the refuge's ecosystem. Kokanee first lay eggs in riverbed gravel, which feed trout and other species, then die after spawning, becoming forage for scavengers.

breaks in the fencing, half circles of riprap rock that provide river access but also prevent river crossings and wandering.

Cottonwood recovery has been tougher in this incredibly dry landscape, where the dam upstream prevents spring floods, so crucial to new cottonwood recruitment. It's the same story wherever dams control flow in the West. Undaunted, Tom and refuge staff continue trying a range of strategies to reestablish cottonwoods, with mixed success and the knowledge that an established, mature cottonwood can live and support life for a hundred years or more; some trees live for two or three centuries in ideal conditions.

Seedskadee's diversion-ditch system from the Green River feeds wetlands for trumpeter swans and other waterfowl. A common problem with diversion ditches are gaps in headgates where fish swim into the ditch and get trapped or flushed into irrigated lands, leading to large die-offs. The refuge's ditch system was leaking at one of the headgates, allowing trout and native whitefish through, where, unable to return to the river, they became an easy meal for herons and pelicans. Tom's Seedskadee team, working with partners Wyoming Trout Unlimited, US Fish and Wildlife Service, US Bureau of Reclamation, and others, developed a specialized fish screen to mitigate this scenario, now commonly used across the West. The advanced custom system works; water can pass through, maintenance is minimal, and thousands of fish are no longer getting flushed through the ditch. Tom is quick to acknowledge his team: "I can't do any of this stuff by myself and give credit to Adam, Katie, Ron, Gene, Colin, and Josh."

Seedskadee is home for Tom and his wife, Shelley, and in Tom's downtime, he's either standing in the river fishing or making outstanding photographs to showcase and tell stories about the refuge and its remarkable wildlife diversity. Tom's photography is an important tool for engagement on this remote wildlife refuge that's known mostly for world-class fishing. With Tom's steady guidance, pragmatic and active management, teamwork, strong partnerships, and focus on giving the ecosystem what it needs, Seedskadee National Wildlife Refuge, "river of the sage grouse," is thriving. ✲

LEFT High in the Wind River Range, rivers of ice form the headwaters of the Green River in west-central Wyoming. In this aerial view, Gannet Peak, at 13,810 feet Wyoming's highest mountain, is ringed by glaciers at the headwaters of the Green River (largest tributary of the Colorado), Gros Ventre River (feeding the Snake and Columbia Rivers), and Wind River (tributary of the Bighorn and Missouri Rivers); farther south in the range are the headwaters of the Sweetwater River (which feeds the North Platte, Platte, and Missouri Rivers). The Wind River Range glaciers, where rivers are born, are receding rapidly. (LightHawk aerial support)

ABOVE Rough-legged hawks are long-distance migrators that like big, open country. "Roughies" spend breeding season in the Arctic and winter across much of the Lower 48 states, preferring open prairie and sagelands in the intermountain West. Roughies can be spotted hovering over open country, hunting for small mammals.

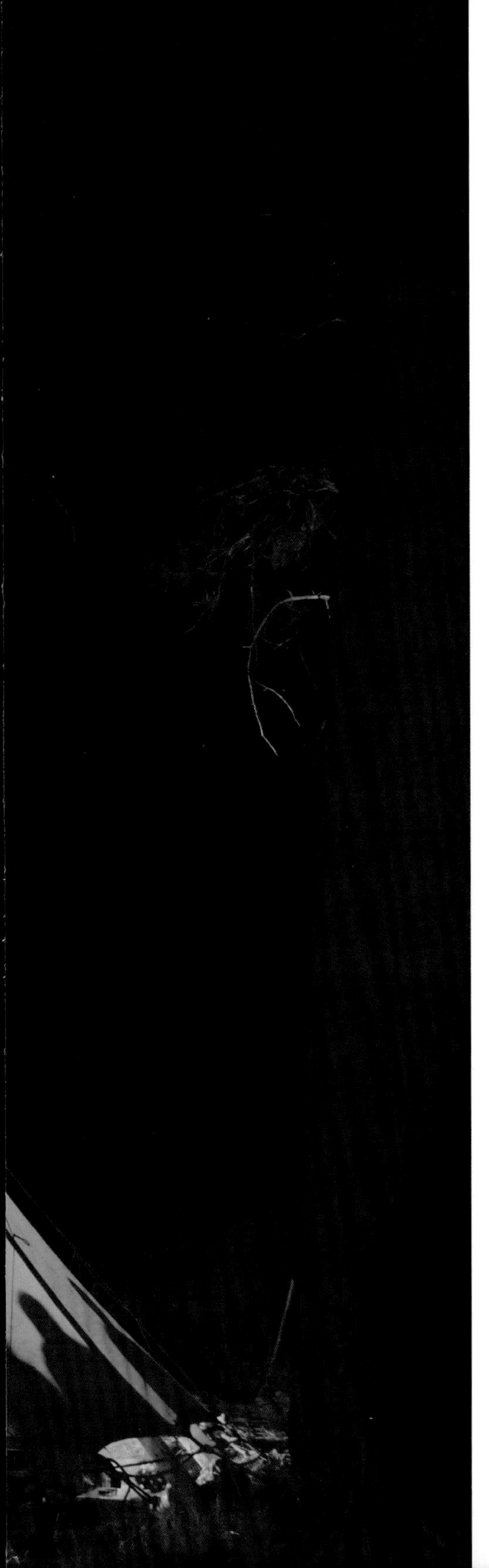

Chapter 3

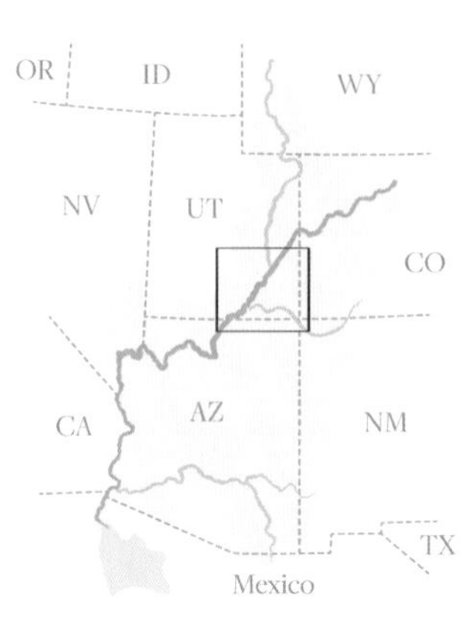

BEARS EARS AND THE SAN JUAN RIVER

Sacred Land, Sacred Water

IN FADING BLUE LIGHT, as darkness settled over ponderosa forest on the Colorado Plateau, a tepee glowed orange, its translucence revealing the silhouettes of elders of the five-tribe Bears Ears Inter-Tribal Coalition encircling the conical structure. A soft drumbeat and faint voices mixed with the tranquility of nightfall in a timeless alchemy of ancient rhythm on sacred grounds. The persistent drumbeat continued, its pulse unchanged as campers retreated for the night to sites dispersed throughout the forest.

Stirring in my solo tent at dawn, when the first birds began chattering, I heard the faint drumbeats like a dream. *Of course they went through the night.*

Before long, people began arriving—many people, gathering from across the region for the Bears Ears running race, a highlight of the annual Utah Diné Bikéyah Summer Gathering. Women, men, cross-country runners, young kids, all ages register for the race and assemble in the meadow for the morning stretch,

Standing at 8,700 feet in elevation, the sandstone Bears Ears Buttes rise above a sagebrush meadow in Utah's Bears Ears National Monument, which encompasses parts of Canyonlands National Park and includes Dark Canyon Wilderness, Cedar Mesa, and Valley of the Gods. The Bears Ears landscape is remarkably diverse, ranging from lush cottonwood- and willow-lined creeks in the canyon bottoms to the high alpine above timberline in the Abajo Mountains. The original inhabitants of this cultural landscape, Indigenous people pass down their language, wisdom, knowledge, ceremony, and a continuum of life through generations.

excitement in the air. The most competitive runners barely touch ground as they carve a corner on their way out to the Bears Ears Buttes; others, including grandmothers with adorable little grandkids, walk-run, laugh, and socialize their way along the course. Many Indigenous people run—in prayer, tradition, culture, community, beauty; for the land, for one another, for causes like epidemic violence against women, for the protection of sacred Bears Ears. This Bears Ears Summer Gathering running race at the 2018 gathering had the air of celebration and jubilation, a joyous morning in Bears Ears.

Geographically, the Bears Ears are two nearly symmetrical sandstone-capped buttes that rise above sagebrush meadows and ponderosa pine forest on the Colorado Plateau in southeast Utah. The protected area of Bears Ears National Monument encompasses parts of Canyonlands National Park, stretching along the Colorado River nearly to Moab in the north and including Dark Canyon Wilderness, Cedar Mesa, and Valley of the Gods. The national monument just touches the San Juan River, a major tributary of the Colorado River, on its southern edge, near the towns of Bluff and Mexican Hat. The land below the buttes

PAGE 89 Elders of the Bears Ears Inter-Tribal Coalition—Navajo Nation, Ute Indian Tribe, Pueblo of Zuni, Hopi Tribe, and Ute Mountain Ute Tribe—held a ceremony that lasted through the night at the 2018 Utah Diné Bikéyah (DEE-nay bee-KAY-ah) Summer Gathering. The Bears Ears Inter-Tribal Coalition describes their collaboration as a "historic consortium of sovereign tribal nations united in the effort to conserve the Bears Ears cultural landscape."

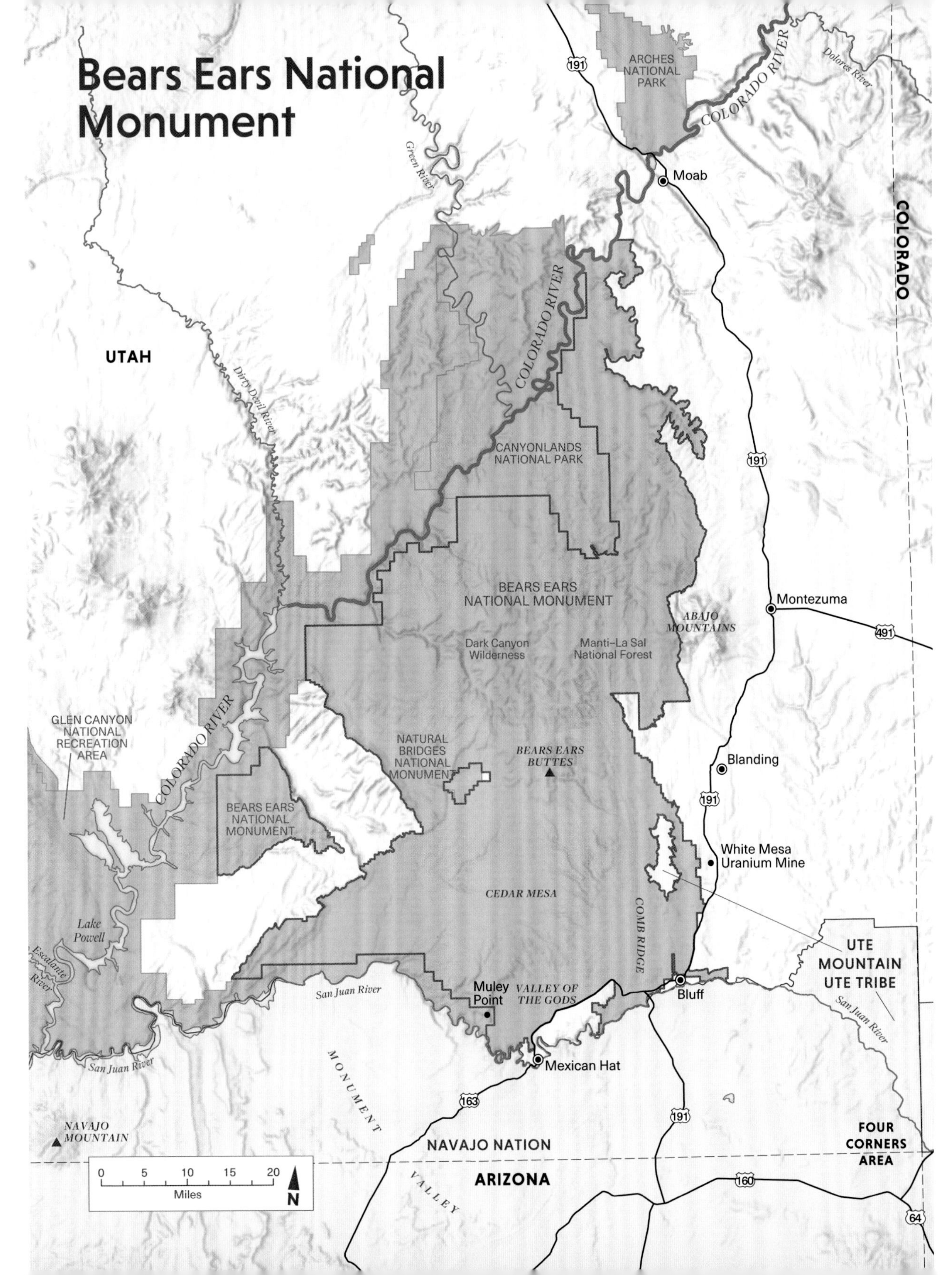

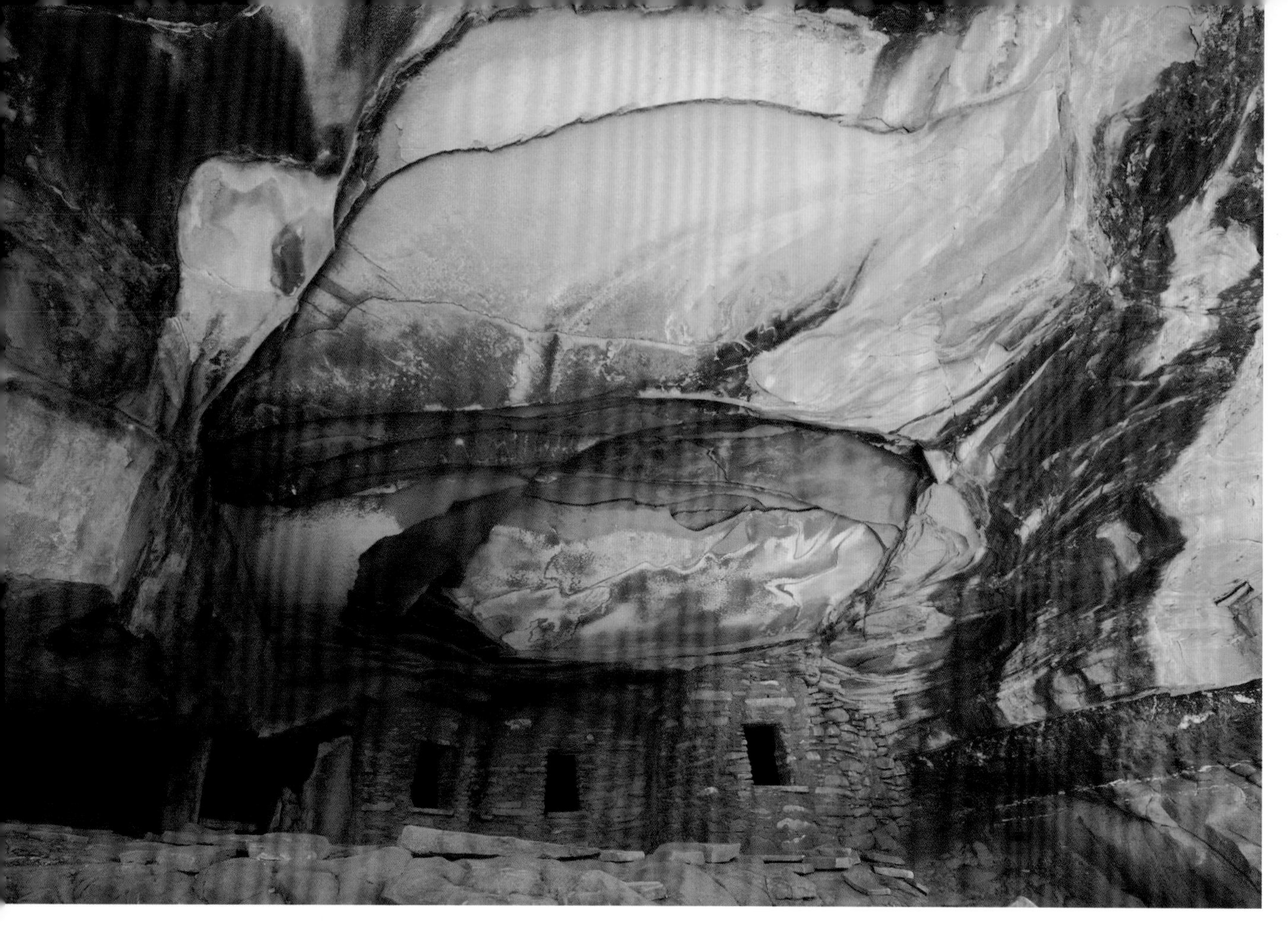

Deep in the canyons of Cedar Mesa and throughout the region, Bears Ears holds sacred places like these cliff dwellings—one of thousands of cultural sites and artifacts of Ancestral Puebloan life. The Ancient Ones invented irrigation in these canyons and thrived for millennia—although there is a colonial word for this Ancestral Puebloan dwelling, it is not used here out of respect for Indigenous people of this landscape who have sacred connections to these lands.

falls off sharply to the south, stretching out with expansive, stunning views across the Colorado Plateau. From Muley Point, just outside of the monument's southwest border, a sweeping, otherworldly vista of Monument Valley, sacred Navajo Mountain, and the goosenecks of the San Juan River unfolds.

Beyond its beauty, this grand view reveals the connectedness of the entire region, the sacredness of ancestral lands, buttes, and spires eroded and shaped by wind, water, and time. The persistent San Juan River has carved deep, entrenched meanders through red rock on its journey to its confluence with the Colorado River in Lake Powell, which also impounds the Escalante, Dirty Devil, and Colorado Rivers. With its headwaters in the namesake southern San Juan Mountains of Colorado, the San Juan is one of North America's muddiest rivers, carrying twenty-five million tons of silt and sediment on its 383-mile journey to the Colorado.

The San Juan River, which drains the remote Four Corners region in Colorado, New Mexico, Utah, and Arizona, is also sequestered in Navajo Reservoir near Durango, Colorado, where 86,000 acre-feet of the river is diverted to Albuquerque and a dozen other projects in New Mexico's Rio Grande watershed via the San Juan–Chama diversion. A thread through time knitting

Ancestral Puebloan culture with modern-day irrigation farming, the San Juan flows through tribal lands of the Ute Mountain Ute, Southern Ute, Jicarilla Apache, and Navajo Nation for more than half of its length. Yet, as noted by the Universal Access to Clean Water for Tribal Communities project, "48 percent of Tribal homes do not have access to reliable water sources, clean drinking water, or basic sanitation."

From where I stand on Muley Point, borders on maps seem meaningless; the immense landscape feels contiguous, intertwined with the continuum of Indigenous life. Ancestral Puebloan people prospered in all of this terrain. From the deep canyons of Cedar Mesa north to the Abajo Mountains, over Comb Ridge and west along the San Juan River, ancient dwellings tucked into cliffs above the floodplain, petroglyphs, and pictograph panels tell a story of a thriving culture and thirteen millennia in these sacred lands. With more than a hundred thousand cultural and archaeological sites—a living record of story, ceremony, irrigation farming of traditional foods, medicine, wildlife richness, and deep knowledge that lives in

Two thousand years of story live in petroglyphs carved into desert varnish at Newspaper Rock State Historic Monument, within the boundaries of Canyonlands National Park and Bears Ears National Monument, Utah.

descendants of the Ancient Ones—Bears Ears and the surrounding landscape are a cultural and spiritual center for Puebloan peoples of the Colorado Plateau.

Many Americans heard of Bears Ears for the first time when President Barack Obama designated Bear Ears a national monument on December 28, 2016—yet this landscape has been sacred to Indigenous peoples from time immemorial. "Rising from the center of the southeastern Utah landscape and visible from every direction," said President Obama, "are twin buttes so distinctive that in each of the native languages of the region their name is the same: Hoon'Naqvut, Shash Jaa', Kwiyagatu Nukavachi, Ansh An Lashokdiwe, or 'Bears Ears.'"

Bears Ears is the first national monument proposed by a coalition of sovereign tribal nations. The five tribes of the Bears Ears Inter-Tribal Coalition—the Hopi Tribe, Navajo Nation, Ute Mountain Ute Tribe, Pueblo of Zuni, and Ute Indian Tribe—came together in 2015 to lead the campaign for protection of Bears Ears. The campaign became a national movement, engaging folks across the country and generating millions of public comments.

The proposed boundaries of Bears Ears came from tribal leaders, as I learned from Cynthia Wilson, who is Navajo Diné, when we met in Monument Valley, Utah, to talk about the Traditional Foods Program. "The original proposal to designate 1.9 million acres for Bears Ears National Monument came from listening to the elders and medicine people who mapped culturally significant plants to protect our narratives," said Cynthia. "In terms of [land] management, traditional knowledge is crucial to protect the entire ecosystem as a cultural living landscape. Our ancestors tended to

The San Juan River carves Navajo Sandstone in the heart of Ancestral Puebloan culture on the Colorado Plateau near Mexican Hat, Utah.

Henry Wilson Sr. fills a 325-gallon water tank in the family's dedicated water truck almost daily—it takes about a half hour for each truck to fill the tank with a garden hose and typically several hours for each fill with multiple trucks queued up. Henry then hauls the water from Gouldings resort's well to the Wilsons' Monument Valley home, where it is distributed to tanks for the family garden, livestock, and home.

these ancient gardens that warrant a special management regime."

Attending the Bears Ears Summer Gathering and being immersed in Indigenous culture for a few days breathed life, beauty, and culture into my own Bears Ears experience. The Summer Gathering transcended prior explorations of Cedar Mesa's spectacular canyons and the surrounding lands in Bears Ears, ancestral touchstones an opening for *seeing* the people of this landscape. *The people are still here. The people have always been here.* And Indigenous people are so generous—I was privileged to witness ceremony (not performance for tourists), celebration of culture, traditional ways, Native language spoken freely, and the sheer joy of gathering on these sacred lands. We were nourished by traditional foods prepared by chefs M. Karlos Baca (Tewa/Nuche/Diné) and Josh Nez (Diné) in the Indigenous Kitchen.

AFTER EXPERIENCING THE SUMMER Gathering and learning of the Utah Diné Bikéyah Traditional Foods Program, I reached out to program founder Cynthia Wilson. The Traditional Foods Program supports families throughout the region growing traditional foods of the Ancestral Puebloans—corn, beans, squash, and now the small but mighty Bears Ears potato—and also funds and distributes 275-gallon water totes. Growing traditional foods is interwoven with access to clean water on tribal lands, where every day many families haul water for horses, sheep, family gardens, and home use.

Bidtah Becker, member of the Navajo Nation and deputy secretary for environmental justice, tribal affairs, and border relations for California's Environmental Protection Agency, is one of the nation's leading tribal water-rights, energy, and environmental-justice practitioners. Testifying before Congress in 2021, Becker described the inequity of water access: "A century ago, the US government invested in modern water and sanitation systems as a means of eradicating waterborne diseases and stimulating economic prosperity, but this government investment in water infrastructure over the past one hundred years has largely bypassed reservations. Today roughly four hundred thousand people—nearly 30 percent of homes in Native communities across the United States—either have inadequate or no access to reliable water and sanitation services. . . . Race is the strongest predictor of water and sanitation access, with Native Americans more likely than any other group to face water-access issues. On my own reservation, it is estimated that up to 40 percent of households do not have clean water to drink or wash with."

Elouise Wilson carefully pours a splash of water on emerging vegetables in the family's traditional-foods garden, where they grow corn, beans, squash, and Bears Ears potatoes. Also working the garden are Elouise's son Brandon Wilson and daughter Cynthia Wilson and Brandon's girlfriend, Jeanne Holiday.

The vista from Muley Point reveals many amazing things and the connectedness of a sacred landscape, taking in the scale of Bears Ears, the goosenecks of the San Juan River, spires of Monument Valley, and sacred Navajo Mountain (out of this frame). The San Juan, a 383-mile-long tributary originating in Colorado's San Juan Mountains that joins the Colorado in Lake Powell, carved an entrenched meander—the famous goosenecks—with the rise of the Colorado Plateau in the last six million years.

At the water-gathering place for Navajo Nation people in Utah's sprawling Monument Valley—a spigot and a plain garden hose up the canyon behind Gouldings resort—Cynthia and I met her father, Henry Wilson Sr., where he was filling a 325-gallon tank in the back of his dedicated three-quarter-ton water truck. It takes about a half hour to fill each water tank from that hose, drawing from the Gouldings well with its attendant "boil water before drinking" sign, and there were six trucks in the queue—a three-hour line to gather water for the day. Every day.

While talking at the water-gathering station, Henry told me, "Sometimes I think I was born to haul water." Henry trucks the water back to the Wilsons' Eagle Mesa home daily, where it is distributed to a number of tanks and transferred to a cistern uphill, from which it flows underground by gravity to the home. During my visit, Cynthia, her mom, Elouise, brother Brandon, and his girlfriend, Jeanne (Jay-AH-nah), were working in their home garden of traditional foods, pouring just a splash of water from five-gallon buckets into cupped red sand holding each individual corn or squash plant, nurturing and trusting there would be good monsoon rains that summer. It's hard work, yet there was laughter and joy in the labor. Looking up north from the garden while taking in the beauty of this landscape, I saw the distant twin buttes of the Bears Ears gracing the skyline. When I returned a month later, squash and knee-high corn were burgeoning, the family enjoying a lovely morning in the garden.

The water-access issue isn't confined to Monument Valley. The Navajo Nation covers 27,413 square miles, and generally wherever homes aren't clustered, tribal members must haul water. Many wells and springs on tribal lands are also contaminated with uranium, and more than five hundred abandoned uranium mines remain in Navajo tribal lands, adding another obstacle in the human right to clean water.

The appalling lack of access to clean water permeates every aspect of Indigenous life, and Native American households are nineteen times more likely than white households to lack indoor plumbing. Inaccessibility of clean water in multigenerational homes disproportionately impacted Native Americans during the 2020 outbreak of the Coronavirus pandemic, when widespread illness and death among Indigenous people was at a rate of three and a half times that of the white population—during those many months when we were all told to wash our hands frequently in hot water for twenty seconds.

When vaccines became available, Native elders were vaccinated first, and the Navajo Nation quickly mobilized and vaccinated more than 90 percent of its population, but the impacts were still severe. While the pandemic raged through tribal communities, in 2020 Bidtah Becker and Anne Castle (see profile), water attorneys and leaders in tribal water rights, developed the Universal Access to Clean Water for Tribal Communities project, which seeks to honor this basic human right owed to Native Americans as part of the promises made in exchange for their ancestral homelands.

AFTER PRESIDENT OBAMA PROTECTED BEARS EARS National Monument in December 2016, President Trump in 2017 eviscerated Bears Ears by 85 percent, Grand Staircase–Escalante National Monument by half, and several other monuments; President Joe Biden then restored Bears Ears and Grand Staircase–Escalante National Monuments in 2021, protecting the original 1.36 million acres designating Bears Ears National Monument. The land didn't become any less sacred in those interim years, and Secretary of the Interior Deb Haaland, who is a member of the Pueblo of Laguna, visited and listened to the five tribes of the Bears Ears Inter-Tribal Coalition prior to reinstatement of national monument status.

Indigenous people see Bears Ears as a place for all people. In June 2022, the US government began a new era by signing a cooperative agreement for the five tribes of the Bears Ears Inter-Tribal Coalition to comanage Bears Ears National Monument. In announcing the partnership, Tracy Stone-Manning, Bureau of Land Management director, said, "This is an important step as we move forward together to ensure that tribal expertise and traditional perspectives remain at the forefront of our joint decision-making for the Bears Ears National Monument." Intertribal coalition members will serve as commissioners in the re-formed Bears Ears Commission and have an important voice in managing the sacred ancestral lands in Bears Ears National Monument.

As of 2022, there is new funding to ensure tribal access to clean water. The November 2021 bipartisan infrastructure law provided $3.5 billion in new funding for tribal water and sanitation systems, with another $2 billion allocated to tribal water settlements. The bipartisan Tribal Access to Clean Water Act would allocate another $2.3 billion to operate and maintain existing water systems and to engineer and construct new systems, fully addressing the essential human need and right to access reliable, clean drinkable water.

I write these words with deep gratitude to all of the Indigenous people who have generously opened their hearts and shared knowledge, tradition, and life. The warm welcome into the beautiful community of the Utah Diné Bikéyah Summer Gathering and the Utah Diné Bikéyah Traditional Foods Program has forever changed my perception of people and place. Thank you for sharing the sacred lands of Bears Ears with all people.

The People are still here, praying for Mother Earth.

EARTH SONG: MY JOURNEY FROM HOME TO BEARS EARS

BY CYNTHIA WILSON

YÁ'ÁT'ÉÉH! (UNIVERSAL GREETINGS IN THIS PLANETARY SPACE) I am present. I am here. I am well.

The Diné (Navajo) language is very descriptive, historically unwritten, and spoken eloquently in lively sayings. The words we speak directly connect us with place and kin through the teachings of our nonhuman relatives who lived long before we have as Earth surface beings. We speak from one voice, as a gift from the Holy People. We put into practice our thoughts, planning, and way-of-life teachings to rematriate the eternal wisdom, leadership, and beauty. We speak as Mother Earth, Father Universe, Protector Mountains, and Water Beings. All who we embody communicates with us, provides us with guidance, comfort, and company, for we are one.

By rematriation, our first connection to life elements comes from the inner spiritual being of our mother. Inside her womb, the flow of her bloodstream provides us with nutrients, air, and water. The sound of her vibrant voice teaches us how to listen and to be patient. Her heartbeat is a soothing rhythm that radiates a sense of belonging and love through our soul. The warmth of her body gives us protection, nourishment, and inner peace. We are made up of the roots of Mother Earth just as we are connected to the umbilical cord. We feed from Mother Earth just like we were fed from our mother. She is our first home.

The foundation of our home is built to emulate the womb of Mother Earth. The female hogan (*hoghan nimazi'*) is an earthen home built of harvested juniper logs, insulated with bark, and enclosed with packs of mud plastered into a round structure of glistening sand. The doorway faces east to ensure we first greet the Sun at dawn, when the Holy People are actively listening. The fire place is at the center and is our teacher and at the heart of all wisdom we bring into the home.

The hogan is held together with nine main posts in a circular form that represents the nine months of pregnancy and the developmental stages of life. The ground has no coverings; our home is directly connected to the Earth's surface so that we maintain kinship from under the soles of our feet. Every day is a journey as we enter the hogan from the east as if we are entering the womb of Mother Earth. We walk clockwise around the fire, in honor and respect to all cardinal directions. Earth songs were derived from the makeup of the hogan. When we sing our songs and speak our prayers in our language, we become a part of the beauty and blessings of the land, water, fire, and air that make up who we are as Earth surface beings.

To the north of our home, in the distance, lie the Bears Ears Buttes. The Bears Ears landscape is important to my family because of the medicines, food, tools, firewood, and everything

Cynthia Wilson holds Bears Ears potatoes in her female hogan, a beautiful structure built with stripped juniper logs from the Bears Ears landscape. The Bears Ears potato is a nutrient-rich, climate-resilient crop grown historically by Ancestral Puebloans and now by their descendants in traditional-foods gardens.

that make up our home. As I travel with my mother, who is an herbalist, rug weaver, traditional cook, and mother of nine children, she always reminds us of our gifts, voice, and ancestral responsibilities as Earth surface beings. She tells us that we are the baby, the child, and the grandchild of Mother Earth, and that is how we relate to our nonhuman relatives.

As we make our way north toward Bears Ears, we first meet the San Juan River. Colonial policies and laws have utilized the river as a line that designates the Navajo Nation on the south side of the river and a state boundary to the north of the river. The San Juan River is known as a male river who at the confluence meets with the Colorado River, known as the female river. I am taught there is always a male and a female side in nature to maintain balance. Just like when grandfather Sun and grandmother Moon face each other, we uphold reverence to pay our respects during that sacred time of them greeting each other.

My mom teaches me that rivers on Earth resemble the veins of Mother Earth. Her veins uphold oxygen and nutrients needed for the soil, vegetation, migratory fish, and animal life that feed from her body. Yet the concepts of property rights and ownership of these rivers are blocked by dams, boundaries, and other structures that degrade the flow of her veins, dehydrating her children. There is no balance when the natural flow of rivers is

TOP The Wilsons—Cynthia, Henry Sr., and Elouise—enjoy a light moment in their Monument Valley traditional-foods garden.

BOTTOM While at the Bears Ears Summer Gathering, I listened to numerous stories of a first hunt in Bears Ears and a first deer with an uncle or grandfather. This mule deer buck in velvet is emblematic of those stories and the idea that for Indigenous people, Bears Ears is life—in heritage, hidden springs, natural medicine, and traditional foods.

A sun break illuminates brilliant red sandstone in Valley of the Gods after a lovely December snowfall in Bears Ears National Monument, Utah.

A grinding stone with tiny corncobs left by the Ancient Ones offers a glimpse into Ancestral Puebloan life in the canyons of Utah's Cedar Mesa. Irrigation agriculture enabled Ancestral Puebloan people to transition from hunter-gatherers to a farming life. The originally proposed boundaries of Bears Ears National Monument were developed by mapping the vegetation plots of Ancestral Puebloan people.

disturbed by such barriers, greed, and development created by humans.

Knowing who I am, as the baby, child, and grandchild of Mother Earth, I try to do my part in maintaining that connection and balance by providing offerings to the river. While crossing the river, I use my voice to give gratitude to the river and humbly ask for precipitation, healing, and a safe journey forward. We greet the river because our offerings to the river travel a long way. When the rivers meet, they give birth to our prayers by providing clouds and moisture to the groundwater, soil, and plants we depend on. The rivers are actively listening, and they have the power of replenishing the Earth to heal from the challenges we are facing with drought and climate change. The plants are listening and I am listening, as the sound of water gives us hope.

This knowledge and practice comes from my grandfather, who instilled in us the importance of reciprocity. He was a prayerful man, a healer, and a medicine person. We would ask for forgiveness for any manmade developments on Earth's surface, such as dams, bridges, roads, and electricity lines that get in the way of the natural order of life. For example, he used to say that Comb Ridge is the backbone of Mother Earth. Today, US Highway 163 runs through the broken ridge. My grandfather would always offer an Earth song as we drove through the broken backbone, as the song would provide a sense of healing and restoration. We would emphasize that we meant no harm and only ask for forgiveness in the destruction of our pathway as we continue our journey forward.

As we get to the twin buttes known as Bears Ears (Shash Jaa'), I pull over at the request of my mother. She steps onto the landscape and shouts as loud as she can, four times in all cardinal directions, "We are here." As if to awaken the female bear's ear canal, who would then shake her back full of gifts, leading us on our way for what we prayed for as we crossed the San Juan River. We always identify ourselves to the land, plants, water, and animals, using our clan system, so that we visit with respect, humility, and gratitude. For we are the baby, child, and grandchild of Mother Earth. When we act responsively, we are heard, valued, and blessed. My mom would tell me that this is a way of giving warning to all relatives on the landscape and to let our ancestors know that we are still here, using our gifts to speak for them and to protect them.

Chief Manuelito was born within the Bears Ears region. He is of the Folded Arms People clan (Bitahnii), which is my maternal clan. My clan relatives share memories of his leadership and role during our toughest time as Diné people being forced on the Long Walk. Before the oppression of the US government, we had stories of puberty ceremonies, hunting rituals, and moving livestock across the San Juan River to Bears Ears, where we also built hogans and sweat lodges. We used to live in tune with the seasons as a way to preserve the landscape. Today, it is a challenge due to the boundaries and margins of our society since ancestral lands have been taken.

As a Diné woman, I have been taught to put 110 percent effort into this colonized society, because that is the only way our voices are being heard in public policy. The protection of Bears Ears is a start. Elders tell me to speak of Bears Ears as if I am Bears Ears. We are one. Bears Ears is us. Bears Ears is listening. The land, water, and universe are calling on us, and we are still here striving to rematriate the Earth for generations to come. We are here. We are here. ✲

CYNTHIA WILSON (Diné) is a tribal member of the Navajo Nation, born and raised in Monument Valley, Utah. She is of the Folded Arms People clan and born in the Towering House clan; her maternal grandfathers are the Running into the Water clan, and her paternal grandfathers are the Red House clan. Cynthia holds a master of science degree in nutrition from the University of Utah. She is attending the University of California–Berkeley's PhD program in environmental science, policy, and management with an emphasis in food sovereignty. Cynthia is currently a Native and Indigenous Rights Fellow, an inaugural cohort of 2021–22 with Harvard Divinity School. She is a cofounder of the Women of Bears Ears, who seek to restore Indigenous women's matrilineal roles and the rematriation of the Earth. She founded the Traditional Foods Program for the Native-led nonprofit Utah Diné Bikéyah, to further its mission to preserve and protect the cultural and natural resources of ancestral Native American lands and bring healing to the Earth. She is currently serving in a consultant role for the Conservation Lands Foundation to conduct outreach to tribes looking to comanage ancestral public lands. Her work encompasses traditional knowledge that addresses the environmental, cultural, nutritional, and spiritual health of the land and the people.

ANNE CASTLE

"Our government appropriated tribal ancestral lands in exchange for a meager promise—that the poor, difficult lands that were forced on them would provide a permanent, livable homeland where tribes could prosper and thrive. That promise is meaningless without water."

A FRIEND AND MENTOR TO ME on this Colorado River journey, Anne Castle is a pragmatic conservationist and expert on the Law of the River and the intricacies of the Colorado River system, someone who cares deeply about clean-water access for Indigenous people. Anne is a Senior Fellow at the Getches-Wilkinson Center for Natural Resources, Energy, and the Environment at the University of Colorado Law School, where she focuses on western water policy issues. She was recently appointed by President Joe Biden as the US Commissioner to the Upper Colorado River Commission. She served previously as assistant secretary for water and science at the US Department of the Interior and before that had practiced water law for nearly three decades.

At the outset of our conversation, Anne tells me she's "flunking retirement." Indeed: she sits on numerous boards, is a policy expert engaged in the workings of the Colorado River system, and is a leader in the Universal Access to Clean Water for Tribal Communities project.

Describing her years as a water lawyer before going to the Interior Department, Anne says, "I practiced law for twenty-eight years, representing all sorts of clients in water issues. And the lovely thing about a water law practice is that you have clients all over the spectrum—from Boy Scout day camps to ski areas to mining companies to environmental NGOs [nongovernmental organizations] and cities. . . . It's a great mix of different individuals and entities all interested in water."

As assistant secretary overseeing the Bureau of Reclamation and US Geological Survey in the Obama administration from 2009 to 2014, Anne and her team had "a wonderful platform for encouraging water conservation and sustainability." At the Interior Department, Anne's team started the WaterSMART program, a comprehensive grant and assessment system that helps to "encourage and incentivize water conservation, accurately assess the status of US water resources, and develop the science for improved forecasts of the availability of water for future economic, energy production, and environmental uses." In 2021 the WaterSMART program included 227 Colorado River Basin projects with a budget of $73.2 million.

One project that excites Anne is the initiative on Universal Access to Clean Water for Tribal Communities, which originated in 2020 when it became clear that tribes were suffering from "a significantly disproportionate incidence of Covid" as compared to the nonnative population. With little or no access to clean water, and multiple generations in many Native American homes, the pandemic's impact was severe before vaccines became

Anne Castle at home in a cottonwood gallery forest on Colorado's Front Range

available. Anne and her colleague Bidtah Becker, Navajo Diné and now deputy secretary for environmental justice, tribal affairs, and border relations at California's Environmental Protection Agency, began talking about the link between Covid and access to clean water, lack of access in Indigenous communities, and the stark differences when compared to communities with access to clean water.

Until 2021, the US federal government had never funded more than 10 percent of the unmet need for water and wastewater systems for tribes. Funding in the Infrastructure Investment and Jobs Act, signed into law by President Biden on November 15, 2021, provided a huge boost for these tribal infrastructure systems: $3.5 billion.

As Anne and I speak about the strain on water resources in the Colorado River Basin, she expresses concern that we have waited too long to address the supply-and-demand imbalance: with reservoirs so low, the options that decision makers have to work with are narrowing. "If we were addressing this supply-and-demand imbalance and our reservoirs were full, we would have a whole bunch more options than we currently have. So that worries me. I think we'll get there. But I'm concerned that it's going to be pretty painful." Still, Anne tells me she's hopeful "because I've seen the key players in this basin come together and address these kinds of [water supply] problems in the past and do it successfully." ✲

Chapter 4

THE MIGHTY COLORADO

Downstream through the Grand

FOR THREE DECADES, I'VE TRIED to grasp the scale and magnificence of the Grand Canyon, on foot, from the air, by boat. Looking back, there's a clear through line to this story, from the first expedition in 1990, when my wife, Marla, and I hiked down from Hermits Rest on the South Rim to the river at Hermit Rapids with friends Alex and Cathy Caldwell. We all staggered under the crushing weight of heavy packs, my own replete with a small French coffee press and a thick Michener book. Marla wasn't my wife yet and my photo kit was a cheap point-and-shoot film camera, but the one unshakable recollection is the feeling of those first few steps, descending beneath the rim of the Grand Canyon. The sensation of leaving overlooks and scheduled life behind, the tactile feel of heat rising from the river below, the sacred experience of time beneath the rim never leaves you.

OPPOSITE Floating the Colorado in the Grand Canyon's inner gorge, as we did in two motorized thirty-plus-foot J-Rig rafts (five pontoons lashed together), profoundly changes people.

RIGHT Native flannel-mouth suckers wrap around a raft in warm, still waters at the mouth of Havasu Creek. The most abundant sucker in the Colorado River system, flannelmouths live up to thirty years and grow to twenty-six inches long in unthreatened habitats.

PAGE 110 The aquamarine artery of the Little Colorado River at its confluence with the Colorado adds life-giving flow to the great river in Arizona's Grand Canyon National Park. At one time, the massive Escalade development planned a tramway to the confluence from a full-scale resort. The Little Colorado confluence is sacred to Indigenous people of the region—the birthplace of Hopi people and current home of Navajo Diné people. (LightHawk aerial support)

I can still feel the nonstop roar of the Colorado from that first Hermit Rapids camp, the visceral power and intention of the great river.

Hiking rim to river is to walk through time as we descended into rock layers marking a third of the earth's history—a vertical mile of magnificent reds and golds, from relatively young 270-million-year-old Kaibab Limestone on the rim down to 1.75-billion-year-old Vishnu Schist basement rocks along the Colorado River, which is still carving the whole masterpiece. Marla and I returned to hike rim to rim on the Bright Angel Trail from the South Rim, and we completed the grueling and spectacularly wild New Hance–Horseshoe Mesa–Grandview loop twice, the only permit we could get for our chance to witness the Colorado River below the rim in all its grandeur.

Prior to rafting the Grand Canyon, longtime partner LightHawk took me on an aerial mission over the Grand Canyon and the confluence of the Little Colorado River with the Colorado, up to Glen Canyon Dam and Lake Powell, and over the Pinyon Plain (uranium) Mine less than ten miles from the South Rim. Each experience reveals something fresh and new, awakening senses while interpreting a world like

A remarkable sight from a river raft on the Colorado, Deer Creek Falls plunges to the river, inviting rafters to stop and explore this magical place in the inner gorge. Deer Creek is sacred to the Kaibab Band of Paiute Indians—tribal youth are taught that their spirit goes to Deer Creek when they die.

Spin, rinse, and repeat: our boat is in the "rinse cycle" while floating and bobbing through Twenty-Three Mile Rapid between walls of Redwall Limestone in Grand Canyon National Park, Arizona.

no other. If descending rim to river is time travel, the inner gorge is a timeless primal force, while the aerial perspective reveals scale, color, context, and our own vulnerability in the thin blue line of the Colorado, lifeblood of the American West.

It wasn't until 2018 that I seriously considered floating the Grand with Audubon Rockies, longtime friends and conservation project partners. We'd rafted the Yampa through Dinosaur National Monument together, drifting through golden canyon walls on Colorado's only free-flowing river, living on river time, while reveling in beauty, lore, adventure, and the bond forged with a shared experience.

The Yampa and Colorado River stories are intertwined by decisions made in the frenetic dam-building era of the 1950s and 1960s, when Echo Park Dam on the Green River just downstream of the confluence with the Yampa was stopped by grassroots conservation raising the question of wilderness values to the American people. The trade-off was that Glen Canyon Dam, which impounds the Colorado River in Lake Powell, would be built instead, from 1956 to 1963, inundating spectacular Glen Canyon while creating the 254-square-mile reservoir, 186 miles long, with a capacity of 27 million acre-feet, the second-largest reservoir in the United States behind Lake Mead, which lies downstream of the Grand Canyon.

THERE'S AN ARC TO EACH RAFT TRIP, A STORY with a distinct beginning, middle, and end. The

LEFT The Vermilion Cliffs catch warm sunrise light from the rim of Badger Canyon, the Colorado River roaring through Marble Canyon in the background. Captive-reared California condors are released at Vermilion Cliffs to range throughout the Grand Canyon region and beyond.

RIGHT This is female condor H9, who fledged in 2018 at this site in Marble Canyon near Navajo Bridge. Although California condors are critically endangered and were almost lost to extinction when all wild individuals were captured for breeding in 1987, today there are now more condors in the wild than in captivity. In Arizona's Grand Canyon region, condors reared in Idaho by the Peregrine Fund are released high on the nearby Vermilion Cliffs. The number-one threat to California condor recovery remains lead ammunition, which poisons carrion that condors scavenge.

prologue is the days leading up, with all of the gathering of stuff, imagining why you'll need waterproof pants and jacket in scorched desert, getting your life in order, then stuffing all of those essentials into a single dry-bag duffel, preparing to get lost off the grid between canyon walls and out of reach for a week or more, placing trust in people you've just met.

For the Grand Canyon expedition, an eight-day trip in spacious, motorized J-Rig boats, we gather in Flagstaff the night before launch to meet the crew for introductions and anxious chatter, then take a morning bus ride to the put-in at Lees Ferry, where fully loaded, lashed boats and crew await. Coleader Abby Burk of Audubon Rockies tells the group to pause and look around, affirming that "water changes everything it touches." Taking a habitat-first approach to bird conservation, Abby and Alison Holloran dreamed up these river trips to immerse conservation-minded folks in some of the most important remaining habitats in the Colorado River watershed and for each of us to be changed by the experience in our own way.

After head boatman B. J. Boyle gives the safety talk while our crew continues well-practiced preparations, B.J. starts us off with a timeless quote from John Wesley Powell's legendary first descent of the Green and Colorado Rivers and their canyons for three months in 1869: "We have an unknown distance yet to run, an unknown river to explore. What falls there are, we know not; what rocks beset the channel, we know not; what walls ride over the river, we know not. Ah, well! We may conjecture many things."

Personal flotation devices are fitted, everyone finds their place, and *whoosh*: boats push off, and the current caresses and sweeps boats, lives, and mountains of gear downstream. The river is already changing us as we drift farther from the put-in. We'll find a rhythm, become a family by day three, and linger at the Diamond Creek takeout 226 river miles and eight days later, wishing for just a little more time with the river.

THE LEES FERRY GAUGE IS ACROSS THE RIVER from the boat put-in above Marble Canyon and the Grand Canyon, marking the official demarcation of the Upper and Lower Basins in the Colorado River system. Of all the gauges on the river, this is the one that records flow from the Upper Basin to the Lower Basin, the gauge that tells us how much water (measured in acre-feet) Lower Basin states Nevada, Arizona, and California will have each season. At this point, the Colorado has absorbed major tributaries—the Green, Yampa, Gunnison, San Juan, Blue, White, Dolores, Eagle, San Juan, and Escalante. The Green has been diverted and impounded at Fontenelle and Flaming Gorge Dams; the Colorado, at Shadow Mountain, Windy Gap, Glen Canyon, and hundreds of other

At the sacred confluence of the Little Colorado River and the Colorado River, the Little Colorado owes its turquoise-blue waters to mineral deposits from Blue Spring, about ten miles upstream.

Forty million people rely on this thin line and the enduring life carried in the Colorado River's flow. From this downstream view from Toroweap overlook on Grand Canyon's North Rim, the river leaves the canyon and enters the engineered plumbing system of dams and diversions to serve industrial agriculture as well as the inhabitants of southwestern cities Los Angeles, San Diego, Phoenix, and Tucson and the Coachella Valley.

tributary dams and diversions. Yet the river's determination to flow downstream, carrying sediment and life in current, is soul stirring as it carves this grandest of canyons—an artist continuing to sculpt a masterpiece in stone. As we pass through buff-white Coconino Sandstone, Marble Canyon just beyond, our scheduled lives fade in the boat's wake.

The river is smooth and glassy as we pass under historic Navajo Bridge (opened to traffic in 1929, providing a new corridor between Utah and Arizona) to enter the soaring white walls of polished limestone in Marble Canyon, so named by Powell. The rolling Badger Creek Rapids make for a gentle introduction to whitewater, with more rapids coming in quick succession: Soap Creek Rapid, Sheer Wall Rapid, House Rock Rapid, each with its own character and lore. Rapids are created when flash floods explode from side canyons, sending rocks and debris tumbling into the inner river gorge, where boulders obstruct flow and narrow the channel, then the river gains speed, building energy, the fast water colliding with slower flow beneath the rapids, forming standing waves and deep hydraulics or "holes" beneath steep drops. As the water speeds up, a glossy, fast-moving V-shaped marker beckons, smooth as a tongue of polished aquamarine glass, entering roiling, rolling, roaring rapids. We enter at the tongue of each rapid, our guide gliding through them in a practiced dance on a dynamic river that is never the same twice.

Camp one is a sandbar at Twenty-Two Mile Wash, and my journal notes Coconino Sandstone towering 1,900 feet overhead. We had started with the Coconino Sandstone seemingly in arm's reach, giving scale to how deep we've dropped in our initiation to the chasm. Deep in the Grand, the inner gorge holds legends and touchstones everywhere—sacred ancestral dwellings, petroglyphs, and granaries of the Ancient Ones, as we're now enveloped in vibrant 340-million-year-old Redwall Limestone. Yellow-breasted chats and yellow warblers call from willow stands, California condors soar a mile overhead, a peregrine falcon lifts off from a sandbar, desert bighorn sheep drink lustily, bellies bloated.

Near river mile 40, we pass under bolts and drilling holes left behind by survey crews for what would have become the Marble Canyon Dam. In the 1960s, two dams were planned for the Grand Canyon—110-foot-tall Marble Canyon Dam and 670-foot-tall Bridge Canyon Dam, each with an attendant power plant—that would have inundated most of the Grand. These bolts that once held scaffolding for dam survey crews still cling to canyon walls as reminders of hubris and folly.

FLOATING THROUGH THESE GORGES, I'M MINDFUL OF those who came before, founders of the modern conservation movement during the 1950s and '60s Bureau of Reclamation dam-building frenzy. In 1952 David Brower of the Sierra Club recruited rabble-rouser Martin Litton to resist Echo Park Dam in Dinosaur National Monument. Litton, first as a *Los Angeles Times* reporter, then founder of Grand Canyon Dories, ran the Colorado River through the Grand Canyon until age eighty-seven and was a lifelong conservationist and wilderness advocate who called Brower the "greatest conservationist of all time." Brower would refer to Litton as his conscience as they first pushed back against Echo Park Dam, appealing to America's wilderness values in a campaign that included the book *This Is Dinosaur: Echo Park Country and Its Magic Rivers*, photographed by Philip Hyde and edited and with a contribution by Wallace Stegner. Howard Zahniser of the Wilderness Society was also instrumental in the Echo Park campaign. Martin Litton's wilderness values are well captured in his words: "What is wilderness? It's mankind's acknowledgment that there is a higher value, a higher purpose. It ceases to be wilderness when we're here. But we are its stewards. It is vital to our souls. It is the source of much of our inspiration."

When Echo Park Dam was stopped, the Colorado River Storage Project, funded and needing storage capacity in the Upper Basin, moved forward with Glen Canyon Dam, which filled from 1963 until 1980, impounding the Colorado in Lake Powell upstream from the Grand Canyon. The construction of Glen Canyon Dam galvanized the modern environmental movement and the general public in an organized resistance when the Marble Canyon and Bridge Canyon Dams were proposed in the Grand Canyon. Brower and Litton, along with Edward Abbey, were among the leaders who ultimately succeeded in saving the Grand Canyon for future generations.

With weather coming on, a rare two-night layover at Nankoweap Creek, mile 53, gives us time to explore Ancestral Puebloan dwellings. Foundations that remain in the floodplain provide a sense of how the small community was arranged and the scale of their farming where Nankoweap Canyon meets the main gorge at Nankoweap Rapid. Nankoweap granaries are 700 feet above the river, windows in a line with a magnificent sweeping view of the Colorado. A solo side hike up Nankoweap Creek unveils a landscape that feels primal and untouched, except for signs of flash flooding: bent willow and stones carefully arranged by ephemeral current along bends in sandy channels where water has receded. Precious rain falls steadily for a little while, so I tuck under a small alcove, mesmerized by raindrops splattering in the little creek, and study the side canyon dotted with skinny young cottonwoods.

Foundations of Ancestral Puebloan dwellings are living history of the floodplain and irrigation agriculture around AD 1050 to 1150. Evidence of corn and pumpkin has been discovered at this Nankoweap Canyon site.

Back on the main river, we drift farther downstream, the turquoise waters of the Little Colorado River joining the Colorado's flow at mile 62. The scene transcends beauty, for it is sacred to Native peoples of Havasupai, Hopi, Paiute, Zuni, Yapavapi-Apache Nation, and Navajo Diné tribes. It is the birthplace of Hopi people and current home of Navajo Diné people. The exquisite color of the Little Colorado is owed to Blue Spring, which bubbles from the ground in the Little Colorado River Gorge, where calcium carbonate turns the Little Colorado turquoise and coats the boulders of these sacred waters in chalky travertine, making for a surreal contrast against towering red walls.

The Little Colorado confluence is a stronghold for native humpback chub, listed as an endangered species in 1967 and subject to a decades-long ongoing recovery effort for endemic fish species of the Colorado River. Named for the prominent hump behind its head, the humpback chub evolved over millions of years in the Colorado's swift current, spawning in warm waters where the Colorado River absorbs the Little Colorado. Dams, with their steady, cold flow and sediment trapping, have degraded riverine habitat and, combined with the loss of peak spring flooding, have left few remaining habitats for native humpback chub, razorback sucker, bonytail, and Colorado pike minnow to recover.

WE FLOAT ON THROUGH SOAKING HORN Creek, Granite, Hermit, and Boucher Rapids. The whitewater is thrilling, and our big boats bounce through one after another in the skilled hands of our guide crew. Late-afternoon camp setup at Crystal Rapid, mile 99, is part of the normal flow by now—form a fire line and move all the gear from boats to shore, arrange tents, set up living room, communicate groover (bathroom) locations—then we disperse and explore new surroundings, darkness climbing up canyon walls. Wandering just downstream from camp, I reach a place where Slate Creek created a gap in the inner gorge, revealing a stunning view to the South Rim bathed in ochre sunset light, Crystal Rapid roiling in aqua blue at my feet. With our small river community well fed, guide and entertainer Jody Tinsley stands by the fire each night to deliver a heartfelt rendering of a Mary Oliver poem he's selected for this place, this moment. Jody also plays guitar and sings into the star-filled night, for us, for the canyon, for reasons all his own.

Continuing downstream, we stop to poke into side canyons and peer from narrow ledges above into Deer Creek slot canyon, mile 137, lined with outrageously green ferns. Standing behind the waterfall, we hear an American dipper singing where the water tumbles from the tiny canyon. By now, we've made peace with sand and blistering heat, and when we reach Lava Falls, mile 180, painting toenails for safe passage seems like a perfectly normal thing to do—for women and men alike as river ritual. So Alison Holloran, in the biggest sun hat you've ever seen, is patiently painting toenails, any color you like, as we float toward Lava's swelling flow, the deep roar intensifying. Lava Canyon lives up to its legend as the most formidable rapid on the journey, with water roaring and roiling everywhere. It's a hoot, navigated skillfully by our crew, yet it's the quiet moments between thrills that stick with me each time I look back on the 226-mile expedition.

It's a short run from the last camp at mile 220 to Diamond Creek Rapid, a quiet stretch of floating on a mirror reflection. As pyramidal Diamond Peak comes into view, our group and crew take a silence break, floating serenely while reflecting on a journey that is profoundly personal—even in a large group. A bus awaits our arrival; some skip stones across the river, and conversation is sparse, in reverence I suppose. Before long, we're at a Route 66 ice-cream tourist trap, strangely reentering the "unreal world" with folks in bright white sneakers.

In the long tradition of river conservation, of bringing people to the river to learn what's at stake and form enduring partnerships, Alison Holloran and Abby Burk have run these trips so there will be more river keepers. There's no hard advocacy conservation message; the river, the outsize magnificence of the canyon, and the experience speak in transcendent ways. We come for beauty, adventure, curiosity, sometimes to heal when we're broken, and no one leaves this spectacular cathedral unchanged. I believe we're changed in part by the totality of the experience and mostly by moving at river's pace day after day, whether methodical or intense in any given moment, whatever the river decides.

There's also the idea of reimagining the possible, that a river running the same course over six million years could create all two-hundred-plus miles of the grandest canyon, of the life the river gives, and of a lifetime of discovery within. By making and returning to this journey in the days and years to come, we reimagine the possible in our own lives, for we are bonded by—and to—the great river.

Water changes everything it touches, including us.

TOP There is nothing like standing along the banks of the Colorado River deep in the Grand Canyon, where we are humbled by the power and roar of the river a vertical mile below the rim. At Crystal Rapid, mile 99 in the Grand Canyon, the glassy tongue of the rapid leads into standing waves that are one of the major challenges to Grand Canyon river runners.

BOTTOM Hiking along ledges above Deer Creek revealed this slot canyon below and a lush world of green, where the sweet song of an American dipper pierced the sound of rushing water.

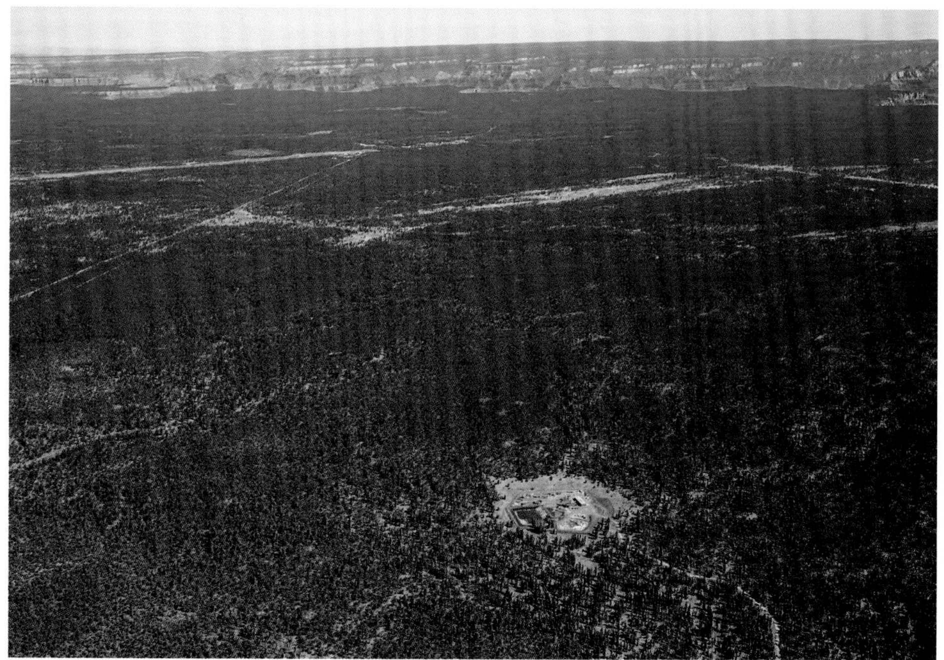

OPPOSITE Morning sun spotlights the Grand Canyon's inner gorge, seen from Hermits Rest on the South Rim, unsettled clouds draping over the rim. As President Theodore Roosevelt wrote on May 6, 1903, "Leave it as it is. Man cannot improve on it; not a bit. . . . What you can do is to keep it for your children and your children's children and for all who come after you."

TOP Beams on the historic Navajo Bridge, downstream from Lees Ferry, Arizona, and the head of Marble Canyon, mimic nature's cliff ledges, giving endangered California condors places to safely roost over the Colorado River. The condor release site at Vermilion Cliffs National Monument is just a short distance away, making Navajo Bridge one of the best places to view wild California condors.

BOTTOM Less than ten miles from the South Rim of the Grand Canyon, the Pinyon Plain Mine (formerly Canyon Uranium Mine) is an active relic of the uranium heyday from 1944 to 1986 that left more than five hundred toxic abandoned mines on Navajo tribal lands. With rights that preceded a twenty-year uranium mining ban in the Grand Canyon region, the Pinyon Plain Mine threatens water quality of Havasu Creek, seeps, and springs that the Havasupai Tribe depends on.

B. J. BOYLE

"You might have to endure a little sand and wind and water, but I think river trips, that experience, is one of the more enlightening adventures that humans can have, partly because you are unplugged."

"DRESS FOR SUCCESS, WE'RE ENTERING THE REAL WORLD," says river guide and trip leader B. J. Boyle of Flagstaff, Arizona, breaking down the plan and preparation for each day with a map, river lore, and a quote for the river ahead from John Wesley Powell's 1869 Grand Canyon exploration journal. The morning routine is well rehearsed: an early coffee call with guests milling around, the crew well into their day, which began at dark-thirty. A big breakfast follows coffee, then the planning meeting and a retreat to tents and tending to the little details of packing everything into a dry bag while preparing for a full day on the water.

I'm intrigued by the river-guide lifestyle and the notion that rivers somehow choose these folks from every walk of life, so I ask B.J. how one becomes a river guide. His journey to guiding began as a Northern Arizona University student, where he studied the Grand Canyon and natural sciences. Working as a backcountry ranger with plans to be a teacher, he detoured from this path "because I got hooked on the river. It's nourishing to my soul, and I love to share this place." He describes beginning as a baggage boatman, rowing the raft that's piled with bags, no people. Then after six trips or so, of being guided by mentors, able to row a boat taking people down the river.

While I'm still grappling with the idea that the river pulls river guides in and holds them there season after season, B.J. offers this: "When people unplug from whatever their life is and they're exposed to a river trip, tapping into and immersing themselves in that world, it becomes very intoxicating for those who are drawn to that kind of lifestyle. It is a lifestyle. It's not for everyone. . . . Just harnessing that feeling—you're constantly surrounded by moving water, all this potential energy, you're basically living off the river, and it becomes an almost symbiotic relationship between you and the river."

OPPOSITE River guide B. J. Boyle is in his element guiding on the Colorado River in Arizona's Grand Canyon.

RIGHT Legendary Lava Falls Rapid engulfs one of our J-Rig boats in the downstream reach of the Grand Canyon on the volcanic Toroweap Fault, where molten rock once oozed down canyon walls and upwelled into the Colorado River channel. In *The Exploration of the Colorado River and Its Canyons*, about his legendary 1869 expedition, John Wesley Powell wrote, "What a conflict of water and fire must have been here! Just imagine a river of molten rock, running down into a river of melted snow. What a seething and boiling of the waters; what clouds of steam rolled into the heavens."

B.J. has guided 219 trips down the Grand Canyon, which he calls "the real world," considering himself a facilitator and "trip adjustor" for the readiness required when the unexpected happens on the water. He was lead guide on our Audubon Rockies trip through the Grand, an expedition with guests and crew in sync throughout. Besides safely navigating everyone downstream, river guides deploy a remarkable skill set every day on the water while providing a world-class experience. Your guide could come from any walk of life, cook gourmet meals, regale the group with tales and history, manage any challenge the river throws at crew and guests, and pluck a swimmer from the current when things go sideways. A great crew makes for an awesome expedition—a group mind develops, with everyone bringing good energy, one organism flowing downstream in bobbing yellow boats.

As we talk about all that goes into putting together a successful expedition, B.J. is quick to say he can't do any of it by himself. "There's a lot of complexities that go into being a trip leader," he says. "You have to look at the gestalt, the whole enchilada, to put a good trip on and consider everything. Consider your crew, the folks, the weather, the water—all that comes into play. And it takes a few years to develop that sense of being able to pull that off or the ability to pull that off flawlessly. But the more you do it, the better you get at it."

B.J. recently retired from more than thirty years of guiding commercial trips and built a Martin Litton–style Briggs boat. He's still on the water regularly, pack-rafting and floating Arizona's Verde and Salt Rivers. ✲

Chapter 5

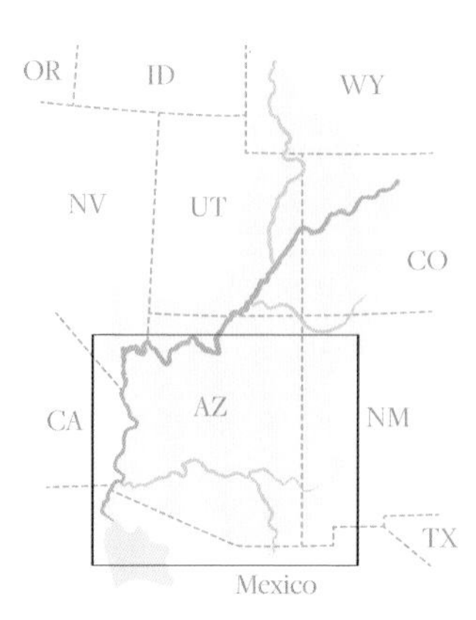

THE GILA HEADWATERS

Pulse of a Wild River

FITZ-BEWW, FITZ-BEWW, FITZ-BEWW!

An olive bird with white belly, no bigger than a medium-size cottonwood leaf, singing for a mate, whirring and calling *fitz-beww* over and over, circled the cottonwood tops above me. I'd watched him for a few days and began calling him Fitz while whispering to coax him lower in the tree canopy. All the other southwest willow flycatchers had apparently gone off to set up nests, so it was just me and Fitz . . . and the yellow-billed cuckoo just overhead. I couldn't see him, but his hard knocking *ku-ku-ku-kddowl-kdowl* reverberated in my head. Called rain crows, yellow-billed cuckoos had just arrived from Central and South America and would set up nests and miraculously mate, hatch, and raise fledglings in just fourteen days, in time for monsoon rains. The air felt cool for an hour or so in early morning, a bit longer in the shade of tall cottonwoods. The smell of loam wafted from a carpet of decaying leaves where a spotted towhee pecked and scratched for grubs a few feet away.

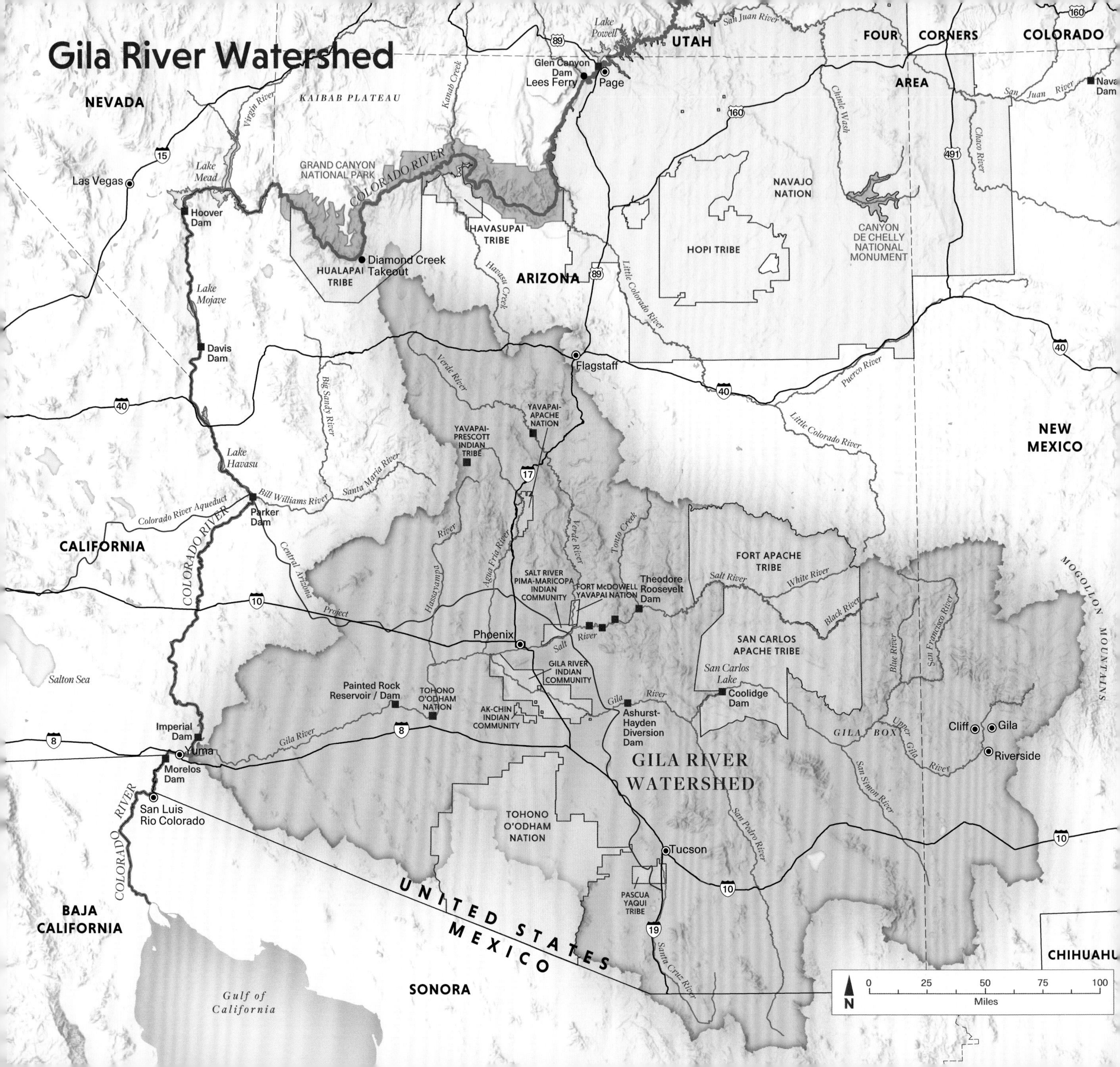

Gila River Watershed
NEVADA
UTAH
FOUR CORNERS AREA
COLORADO
ARIZONA
NEW MEXICO
CALIFORNIA
BAJA CALIFORNIA
SONORA
CHIHUAHU
UNITED STATES
MEXICO
KAIBAB PLATEAU
GRAND CANYON NATIONAL PARK
COLORADO RIVER
Lake Powell
San Juan River
Glen Canyon Dam
Lees Ferry
Page
Las Vegas
Lake Mead
Hoover Dam
Virgin River
Kanab Creek
Diamond Creek Takeout
HUALAPAI TRIBE
HAVASUPAI TRIBE
Havasu Creek
NAVAJO NATION
HOPI TRIBE
CANYON DE CHELLY NATIONAL MONUMENT
Chinle Wash
Chaco River
Navajo Dam
Little Colorado River
Puerco River
Flagstaff
Lake Mojave
Davis Dam
Lake Havasu
Verde River
Big Sandy River
Santa Maria River
Bill Williams River
Parker Dam
Colorado River Aqueduct
Central Arizona Project
YAVAPAI-APACHE NATION
YAVAPAI-PRESCOTT INDIAN TRIBE
Hassayampa River
Agua Fria River
Tonto Creek
SALT RIVER PIMA-MARICOPA INDIAN COMMUNITY
FORT McDOWELL YAVAPAI NATION
Theodore Roosevelt Dam
FORT APACHE TRIBE
Salt River
White River
Black River
Phoenix
SAN CARLOS APACHE TRIBE
San Carlos Lake
Coolidge Dam
Blue River
San Francisco River
MOGOLLON MOUNTAINS
GILA RIVER INDIAN COMMUNITY
Painted Rock Reservoir / Dam
TOHONO O'ODHAM NATION
AK-CHIN INDIAN COMMUNITY
Ashurst-Hayden Diversion Dam
Gila River
GILA BOX
Upper Gila River
Cliff
Gila
Riverside
Imperial Dam
Yuma
Morelos Dam
San Luis Rio Colorado
Salton Sea
GILA RIVER WATERSHED
San Simon River
San Pedro River
Tucson
PASCUA YAQUI TRIBE
Santa Cruz River
Gulf of California
0
25
50
75
100
Miles
N
15
40
8
10
17
19
89
160
491

A chipping sparrow, common to brushy areas like riparian floodplains, nestles in autumn sycamore on The Nature Conservancy's Gila River Farm.

PAGE 130 The upper Gila River flows from southwest New Mexico's Mogollon Mountains through autumn golds and oranges of cottonwood and sycamore in Arizona's Gila Box Riparian National Conservation Area. The undammed upper Gila holds stunning wildlife diversity and abundance, owed to the river running wild and free with a natural flood regime.

My perspective was an opening in a thick cottonwood gallery forest, a ballroom encircled by tall trees, with new growth poking through to catch the sun's rays when the trees swayed in the wind. The upper Gila (HEE-la) River was just west, off my right shoulder and fifty yards beyond the forest edge. Local naturalist Mike Fugagli had kindly come out from Silver City, New Mexico, to show me a couple of spots downstream from the old Iron Bridge on The Nature Conservancy's Gila River Preserve, established in 1982 with the first land acquisition. The Iron Bridge Conservation Area, downstream from the town of Cliff, is co-owned by TNC with the New Mexico Department of Game and Fish. Although I'd been here before, I needed guidance to witness the endangered flycatchers and threatened cuckoos. It's one thing to hear the birds and another thing altogether to see and photograph them in leafed-out cottonwood forest. Mike had just spent a week with students trapping and tagging songbirds here and, as he left, said, "Take care of yourself; it's going to be a tough week." Mike was referring to the blistering heat, with forecasted daily highs of 106 to 108 degrees Fahrenheit, while my Colorado home forecast was peaking at over 100 the same week. There was nowhere in the West to hide in the third week of June 2021.

The flycatchers, cuckoos, and 80 percent of all vertebrate species of the Southwest are here on the

The signature of the wild upper Gila is glorious cottonwood forest seemingly pouring from the Mogollon Mountains. The Gila River channel is marked by golden autumn cottonwoods, which need to have their toes (roots) in water, with orange sycamores dotting the ephemeral and "flashy" (prone to flash floods) Mogollon Creek. This free-flowing oasis in the Sonoran Desert of southwest New Mexico provides the right habitat for more than two hundred species of birds and a broad range of wildlife.

upper Gila in southwest New Mexico because here it's still a wild river, with a natural flood regime. The Gila's birthplace in the Mogollon Mountains of southwest New Mexico, 650 river miles from its confluence with the Colorado River near Yuma, Arizona, is the ancestral homeland of Mogollon Culture, their interlinked cliff dwellings built in natural caves preserved high in the Mogollons at Gila Cliff Dwellings National Monument. The Mimbres, a branch of the Mogollon Culture, lived along the Mimbres River to the east and occupied segments of the Rio Grande and Gila River. There are ancestral Mimbres sites near the Iron Bridge and scattered on terraces throughout the upper Gila floodplain.

In more recent times, this is Aldo Leopold country, where the father of wildlife ecology and wilderness developed his ideas of a "land ethic." Locally, folks simply call the legend "Aldo," as you would a dear friend. As he wrote in *A Sand County Almanac*, Leopold firmly believed that "when we see land as a community to which we belong, we may begin to use it with love and respect." While working for the US Forest Service in New Mexico, with wildness disappearing in the West, Leopold sought to "protect the blank spots on the map." Leopold's vision and lobbying to protect the entire Gila River watershed led to the designation of the Gila Wilderness in 1924 as the world's first wilderness area. The Gila Wilderness is massive at 558,065 acres, and together with the Aldo Leopold Wilderness to the east and Blue Range Wilderness to the northwest, more than 792,000 acres are protected as wilderness in the Gila National Forest.

SOUTHWEST RIVERS WERE A MYSTERY TO ME when I first traveled to the Gila in 2017, stoked by enthusiasm for the Gila by Dr. Mary Harner and her husband, Dr. Keith Geluso, while we were all at the Greater Prairie Chicken Festival in the Nebraska Sandhills. Mary is an advisor for Platte Basin Timelapse, which studies watersheds in motion, based out of the University of Nebraska–Lincoln. Mary studies the ecology of the upper Gila, Middle Rio Grande, and Platte River systems. Keith is a mammalogist, interested in bats, rats, and anything that crawls, slithers, or flies in the Gila. Professors at the University of Nebraska–Kearney, Mary and Keith were earning their PhDs at the University of New Mexico when they met while both were researching, and falling in love with, the Gila. While at the Greater Prairie Chicken Festival, we made plans to gather on the Gila, where I would meet Martha Cooper, The Nature Conservancy's (TNC) Southwest New Mexico Program manager and Freshwater Program manager. She would probably tell you her job is to build community.

TOP A pair of sandhill cranes lift off in pasture grass on The Nature Conservancy's Gila River Preserve in the upper Gila River floodplain. A small population of sandhill cranes, most likely of the Rocky Mountain flock, uses the upper Gila River valley as winter habitat.

BOTTOM Collared peccaries, also known as javelinas, roam Southwest floodplains, rooting for prickly pear cactus, tubers, grubs, and small insects. Peccaries are mostly nocturnal in summer, when this individual came grubbing through my camera trap in riparian forest near the upper Gila River.

Martha, her husband, Tom, and their daughter, Frances, are stewards at TNC's Gila River Farm, with water rights in southwest New Mexico's Cliff–Gila Valley community. An irrigation ditch that's perfect for swimming flows through the front yard. It's an easy stroll from here to walk an Arizona black walnut–lined lane out to the duck pond, or you can continue to the cottonwood-lined edges of the upper Gila, where you can wander far with the broad Mogollon Mountains in full view.

TOP A passing storm's curtain of rain is illuminated by the setting sun over floodplain farms in this south-facing view of the upper Gila River valley.

BOTTOM Mature cottonwoods in peak autumn gold arch over the upper Gila River in the Gila Box Riparian National Conservation Area. Imagine for a moment standing shin deep in the channel, feeling the pulse of a wild river coursing through your body. We too are made of water and pulse, our lives owed to rivers: lifeblood.

TNC purchased the Gila River Farm and established the Lichty Ecological Research Center in 2000 with primary goals of protecting habitat and wild biodiversity, understanding that having a presence in the community and participating in water-management decisions is critical for conservation. With Martha's leadership, TNC has a seat at the table with local irrigators, is demonstrating sustainability and compatibility with (hay-field) river agriculture, has created a wetland demonstration project, and promotes and supports science, education, and conservation partnerships through the Lichty Ecological Research Center.

As I walked a dry river channel with Mary and Martha one gorgeous summer evening, Mary pointed to cobble in the riverbed, and we had a teaching moment about the interstitial gaps between rocks that hold aquatic life and how Southwest rivers sometimes flow below the surface because it's easier than flowing over a sandy channel. The river wasn't dried up yet; it was simply running through sandy, gravelly alluvial material, finding the easiest way to continue downstream.

Upstream, the river flows through the Gila Wilderness, where tall canyon walls through which the river flows recede as it emerges from the Mogollon Mountains and rolls out onto the floodplain, then appears and disappears through the alluvial valley bordered by farmlands downstream. It's a "flashy" river, prone to mighty flash floods, a late-summer unleashing of explosive energy down from the mountains. In a good summer, there will be a number of violent monsoon events when water explodes from the headwaters in a torrent, sometimes carving new channels and remaking the watercourse. Sediment is flushed from river rock and pushed onto the floodplain, creating new habitat for willow, cottonwood, and sycamore recruitment, woody vegetation where wildlife thrive. Aquatic insects, indicators of a healthy river system, flourish in voids between river rocks, wetlands are recharged, and generations of cottonwood gallery forest are flooded. Undammed, the upper Gila flows free and wild through the headwaters and out of the mountains into the floodplain.

Endangered southwest willow flycatchers find refuge in the healthy cottonwood-willow structure along the upper Gila River of New Mexico. Just a bit bigger than a cottonwood leaf, these flycatchers were listed as endangered in 1995 because of habitat destruction due to development, cowbird nest parasitism, livestock grazing, and other threats. This individual flew around the canopy of the cottonwood gallery forest in June calling *fitz-beww, fitz-beww, fitz-beww* to attract a mate. The upper Gila supports a robust breeding population.

The New Mexico towns of Gila and Cliff are centers of an extended community spread across the broad valley, where flood-irrigated fields border a wide riparian corridor along the Gila, humble homes sprawled out on the edges. Cattle ranches surround the Cliff–Gila Valley, bringing together a mix of people as diverse as the wildlife attracted to a wild river running free through the desert landscape. Those who aren't multigenerational ranchers come for a lot of reasons, and I've gathered it's their grit, the river, and the spirit of community that hold them here. Some will simply say, "I don't know, there's just something about this place." I'd give the same answer for why I keep going back.

As the upper Gila leaves the narrow canyon and flows into the Cliff–Gila Valley, the river spills onto the floodplain through an arching cottonwood gallery. Right there, where a river gauge measures flow in cubic feet per second, is where a dam would have been built, the reservoir impoundment backing up into the Gila Wilderness. The worst of it would have been the destruction of downstream habitat on the last free-flowing river in New Mexico, one of the wildest and most biodiverse places in the American Southwest. The Hooker Dam, or "suitable alternative," and associated diversion structures were proposed and authorized under the Colorado River Basin Project Act in 1968 as a component of the Central Arizona Project. More contentious proposals followed over five decades, each contested by conservationists, and none of the proposals were economically feasible. The 2004 Arizona Settlement Act between New Mexico and Arizona allowed the state of New Mexico to divert and use an additional 14,000 acre-feet of Gila River water annually—an acre-foot supports one to two families for a year. It's paper water anyway, because in most years there isn't an extra 14,000 acre-feet in the system. You can't blame ranchers and farmers for wanting water security, however unaffordable, or other folks for wanting a flowing river for wildlife and to soothe our souls.

After decades of controversy and protracted resistance over diverting the upper Gila from the headwaters, the cost-benefit analysis never made sense. In 2021 New Mexico Governor Michelle Lujan Grisham signed House Bill 200, prohibiting any more spending on a dam or diversion in the Gila headwaters. The project was shelved, redirecting $91 million in southwest New Mexico water funding toward higher-priority projects providing long-term water security.

What is this last wild river worth?

ONE STILL NIGHT UNDER A FULL MOON, I STOOD ON THE Iron Bridge in TNC's Gila River Preserve listening to the Gila's burbling voice. Headlamp off, my eyes recalibrated to darkness, revealing contours of river's edge and the dendritic gestures of cottonwoods lining the river, moonlight faintly painting riffles in the blue of night. It seems so simple: just go to the river to be at peace, to breathe, to find a center; to forge our own relationship with the river.

Dr. Keith Geluso took me out for night work, studying biodiversity in the Gila headwaters floodplain. Desert heat wanes at dusk, and night is a time for wild imagination, when bats, owls, snakes, kangaroo rats, bears, wildcats, and javelinas take over. In the floodplain near the Gila Box, Keith set Sherman traps: a tiny trail of seeds leading to a hinged trap door. Elf owls' *pe pe pe pe pe pe pe pe pe pe* calls rose and descended from mature sycamores interspersed with cottonwood. We poked under bridges for bats and drove slowly to avoid running over snakes, stopping to move them off the road. Keith was also educating students from Fort Hays, Kansas, who affectionately called him "Dr. G." A mist net set over a stock tank caught bats one after another, students gathering around for an intimate in-hand teaching session by headlamp—pallid bats, western red bats, hoary bats, big brown bats, several species of *Myotis* (mouse-eared bats), Mexican free-tailed bats—with the bats released afterward, crickets playing background music. The Sherman traps caught deer mice and Ord's kangaroo rats—a long tail, comically big feet, and powerful legs enable the rats to leap nine feet to avoid predators. Not coincidentally, Dr. G. loves kangaroo rats, maybe most for their seed-carrying furry cheek pouches, their giant feet, their role as seed dispersers in the ecosystem, but also as food for owls, badgers, snakes, coyotes, bobcats, and other nocturnal predators.

Until you know the upper Gila, it's hard to imagine the river's critical importance for migrating birds and wild biodiversity; after all, the Gila looks like a small stream in these headwaters. Heck, you can even walk a dry channel and wonder where the river went. I went walking one summer afternoon with Tom Cooper, Martha's husband, who's been woven into the Gila community fabric since 1989. Back then, cows were on the floodplain, trampling vegetation, collapsing banks, wallowing in water holes, leaving the river "cowed out." Tall and rangy, Tom flowed over the floodplain, removing

TOP Dr. Keith Geluso plucked this beautiful bull snake from a road in the Cliff–Gila Valley and moved him to safety. Keith drives slowly, very slowly, in snake season for good reason.

BOTTOM First spotted in an apple tree on The Nature Conservancy's Gila River Farm, this coatimundi moved to eating desert hawthorn berries over the irrigation ditch. White-nosed coatis are in the family Procyonidae, related to raccoons and ringtail. They are mostly daytime foragers that are very fond of fruit; excellent climbers, they use their long tails for balance. Coatis often travel in troops of four to twenty-five females with young. Their range in the Colorado River watershed is southwest New Mexico and southeast Arizona, extending into central Arizona and Mexican Sonora.

In June, as northern cardinal males chased females at high speed through brush on The Nature Conservancy's Gila River Farm, this beautiful male paused in the forest along the irrigation canal, then flew off to find a mate.

his shoes and walking barefoot through the river channel. I did too, my city feet aching. Long after the community had come together to remove cattle from the floodplain in the late '90s, Tom parted thick willow taller than head high, telling me it's all from a new channel carved by the river the previous year. You can drive over the river bridge to get to the Gila townsite, but walking is far more interesting and direct. We met neighbors exchanging news by word of mouth: kids' birthday-party invites, an upcoming stuccoing party to seal a new home. The Gila River mosaic of wilderness, grassland, ranches, human and wild communities, and biodiversity is all knitted together by a single thread—a healthy river system with a natural flood regime. Somehow people with diverse interests, drawn here by the river, are figuring it out.

Downstream, the Gila dips south and then west, running free into Arizona, where it gets wrung out in cotton fields and impounded behind dams, the story of our Southwest rivers. The river irrigates alfalfa and cotton farms across Arizona in Pinal and Maricopa Counties, dewatered on its journey to meet the

Colorado River. I couldn't locate the confluence near Yuma, instead finding myself in a tangle of salt cedar and cracked mud, peering up a choked channel where a bathtub-size puddle held a chattering belted kingfisher and a single snowy egret. Water and life. Our anthropogenic thirst, thirsty crops, and climate change have completely altered the hydrology of the American Southwest, yet we have the upper Gila as critical habitat and a reference river for what's possible, a place to shout "Look what we have!"

This stunning river, free-flowing in its wild upper reaches, still has much to teach us, and we don't fully know the future peril of global heating impacts as the Mogollon Mountains shift from a winter snow regime to rain, as massive wildfires pose threats to riverine habitat, clogging streams and rivers with black ash that kills fish. Yet the endangered southwest willow flycatcher and yellow-billed cuckoo still come to the upper Gila for tall willow and ancient cottonwoods; endangered fish—loach minnow, Gila topminnow, spike dace minnow, and Gila trout—still swim native waters. Sandhill cranes still come in autumn to the Gila Valley, calling and flowing in primordial rhythms while gaining weight in farmers' pastures for spring migration. In violent monsoon events, the upper Gila still carves new channels, unleashing life across the floodplain.

AS MY TIME WITH FITZ, THE SOUTHWEST willow flycatcher, wound down, I had a few glimpses of him lower in the tree canopy and felt joy just knowing this short stretch of the upper Gila is a stronghold for these endangered birds. I stepped into the sunlight and walked toward the river, a common black hawk calling loudly from the top of a gnarled old cottonwood. Yellow-breasted chats, northern cardinals, vermilion flycatchers, and so many unseen birds were buzzing and chattering when—*kerplunk*!—a beaver appeared from a bank hole, a Southwest beaver lodge on a flashy river. The beaver swam circles as the black hawk called, and in that moment everything was as it should be. Decades of conservation work, wide and deep, conservation in community, saved the upper Gila. The river's wild soul runs free.

TOP Beavers on the flash flood-prone upper Gila build their lodges in riverbanks. On the edge of the cottonwood gallery forest where I witnessed southwest willow flycatchers and yellow-billed cuckoos were beaver riverbank holes among the long roots of tall cottonwoods. Overhead, a common black hawk called in high-pitched whistles from a lofty branch of a stately cottonwood as this beaver swam in lazy circles, the willow in the riparian oasis buzzing with songbird chatter.

BOTTOM Phainopepla, often called the black cardinal, also silky flycatcher, are common in brushy desert washes and oak and sycamore woodlands of the desert Southwest. A singular species, phainopepla favor mistletoe in winter and berries from spring through fall. This male was one of many that arrived on the Gila River Farm to gorge on elderberries one July morning.

TOP A tree fungus hangs on a cottonwood trunk in the upper Gila River floodplain of New Mexico.

BOTTOM On a walking tour of the Gila River floodplain with Tom Cooper, we encountered Doug Simon standing barefoot in the shin-deep cold river with three burros. Doug, whispering sweetly to one of the animals, asked about this story, so I talked about the Living River idea. Doug looked me in the eye and said, "Just tell people you love her." I love you, Gila River.

OPPOSITE High in the Mogollon Mountains near the Gila's headwaters in the Gila Wilderness, Gila Cliff Dwellings National Monument protects homes of the Mogollon people, who occupied these dwellings in the late 1200s. Mogollon people were hunters and gatherers who farmed mesa tops and along the West Fork of the Gila River. Approximately forty to sixty individuals lived in dwellings in five caves with forty-six rooms.

MARTHA COOPER

"The upper Gila River is still wild. Not as in 'wilderness' wild, but wild and powerful and untamed. Undammed."

SITTING RIVERSIDE BY THE UPPER GILA RIVER GAUGE in the Gila Box, Martha Cooper is reflective, telling me, "I've had the honor of working and living here for sixteen years, and I joke that it's my own occupy movement. I'm not leaving." Martha is The Nature Conservancy's (TNC) Southwest New Mexico Program manager and Freshwater Program manager. This is the first time we've met since the proposed dam and subsequent diversion structures were shelved in 2021. The dam would have been raised where Martha is sitting.

She explains how the 2004 Arizona Settlement Act provided federal funding to support diverting up to 14,000 acre-feet from this location, the reservoir extending into the Gila Wilderness, and that the right to develop still exists, but that funding will now be used more sustainably for priority water projects and long-term water security in the region. About the diversion, Martha says, "We've spent all these years fighting to protect the Gila—the diversion would have industrialized and dewatered the river, degrading habitat in perpetuity." Martha adds that the abundant aquatic insects on the upper Gila are indicators of the river's health and water quality and that "the most amazing thing about the Gila is, there's no dam upstream and no downstream impoundments in New Mexico."

Unlike rivers below dams, in this river's headwaters there are no visible signs of invasive plants choking native flora, thanks to the big monsoon floods that scour the floodplain and carve new channels in late summer. Talking about what's at stake—habitat for the endangered loach minnow and spike dace minnow, a robust population of endangered southwest willow flycatchers, wildlife richness tied to the dynamic nature of a wild river—Martha says, "Riparian species like cottonwood, willow, and sycamores need to have their feet in groundwater, which is sort of what defines them." Our western dam dilemma of restoring woody vegetation for riparian ecosystem health is just that—how to keep trees rooted in water in the absence of spring floods.

TNC's Gila River Preserve protects 1,200 acres in the riparian corridor of the upper Gila floodplain, including a farm with water rights. Farmers and ranchers who own water rights in the valley are called "irrigators," and because TNC is a landowner with water rights, Martha attends irrigators' meetings to "hear what people want and why they care about the river." Martha sees her work as an opportunity to "develop much stronger relationships with my neighbors and irrigators in the valley" and tells me it's "rewarding working with people who share a love of place."

With the Hooker Dam and diversion of the headwaters to Arizona shelved, the irrigators were presented with a range of options to redesign the upper Gila River's local agricultural diversions for efficiency while maintaining instream river flows. The irrigators' engineers worked with TNC engineers, and the irrigators ultimately chose the natural, most environmentally compatible channel design in keeping with stream integrity, a remarkable outcome after decades of pushing for an impoundment and diversion.

Martha recalls the time when she and her husband, Tom, with their daughter, Frances, and river dog Tessa, decided to live on TNC's Gila River Farm—of building forts with flood debris, plunging in swimming holes, and hearing the incredible "geomorphology observations" of a toddler on a river adventure, "the gift" of exploring it all with Tom and Frances.

Cliff–Gila Valley folks are tethered to New Mexico's only free-flowing river, pitching in for one another and the upper Gila. There's a long, rich history of community building embodied in Martha's work and in the shared gift of place. ❂

OPPOSITE Martha Cooper at the Gila headwaters where, thanks to her and community efforts spanning decades, the Gila flows freely where a dam and diversion were once planned.

RIGHT Martha Cooper (at left) and Dr. Mary Harner walk a dry channel in the Gila River floodplain with river dog Tessa. The Gila carves new channels during major monsoon events, part of the natural process of remaking and renewing the river. Water, which seeks the easiest path, will also subvert, flowing deep beneath the surface in the alluvial aquifer.

Chapter 6

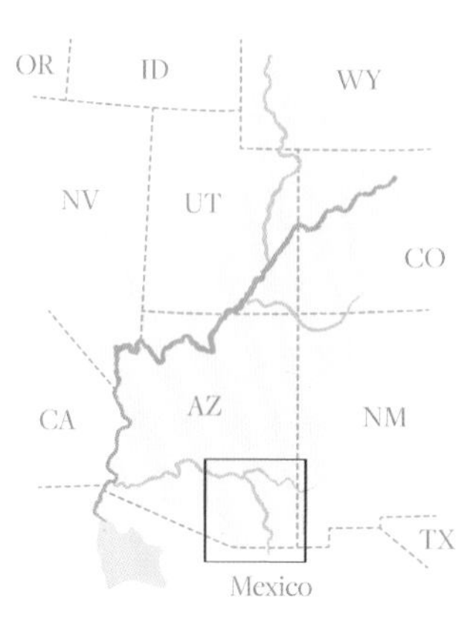

THE SAN PEDRO RIVER

Deep Water

STANDING IN WAIST-HIGH GOLDEN GRASSLAND atop Coronado Peak, namesake of Arizona's Coronado National Memorial, I watched as the winter sun fell rapidly over the Sierra Madres in the state of Sonora, Mexico. I traced the border wall east until it melted into the horizon, then found a thin line of cottonwood forest marking the serpentine course of the San Pedro River. Mexico lay just to the south over my right shoulder, a few thousand feet below my Huachuca Mountains "sky-island" aerie. As border towns Hereford, Bisbee, and Naco lit up in fading dusk, so did the Cananea copper-mining town on the Mexico side of the border, splashes of bright light in the vast blackness of the Apache Highlands, topped by mountain ridge silhouettes. Wind and the persistent rattle of sun-baked, waist-high grass were the only sounds, a peaceful place.

More than fifty sky-island mountain ranges rise from southern Arizona sacaton grasslands and the Sonoran Desert; another thirty-plus sky-island ranges stretch across the Mexican states of Chihuahua and Sonora. Created by expansion and uplift between five and fifteen million years ago and shaped by volcanic eruption, magma and ash flows, folding, and faulting, sky-island mountains are life-giving oases, jewels towering over vast desert grasslands. When moist monsoonal summer air masses from the Gulf of California collide with sky islands, the air rises

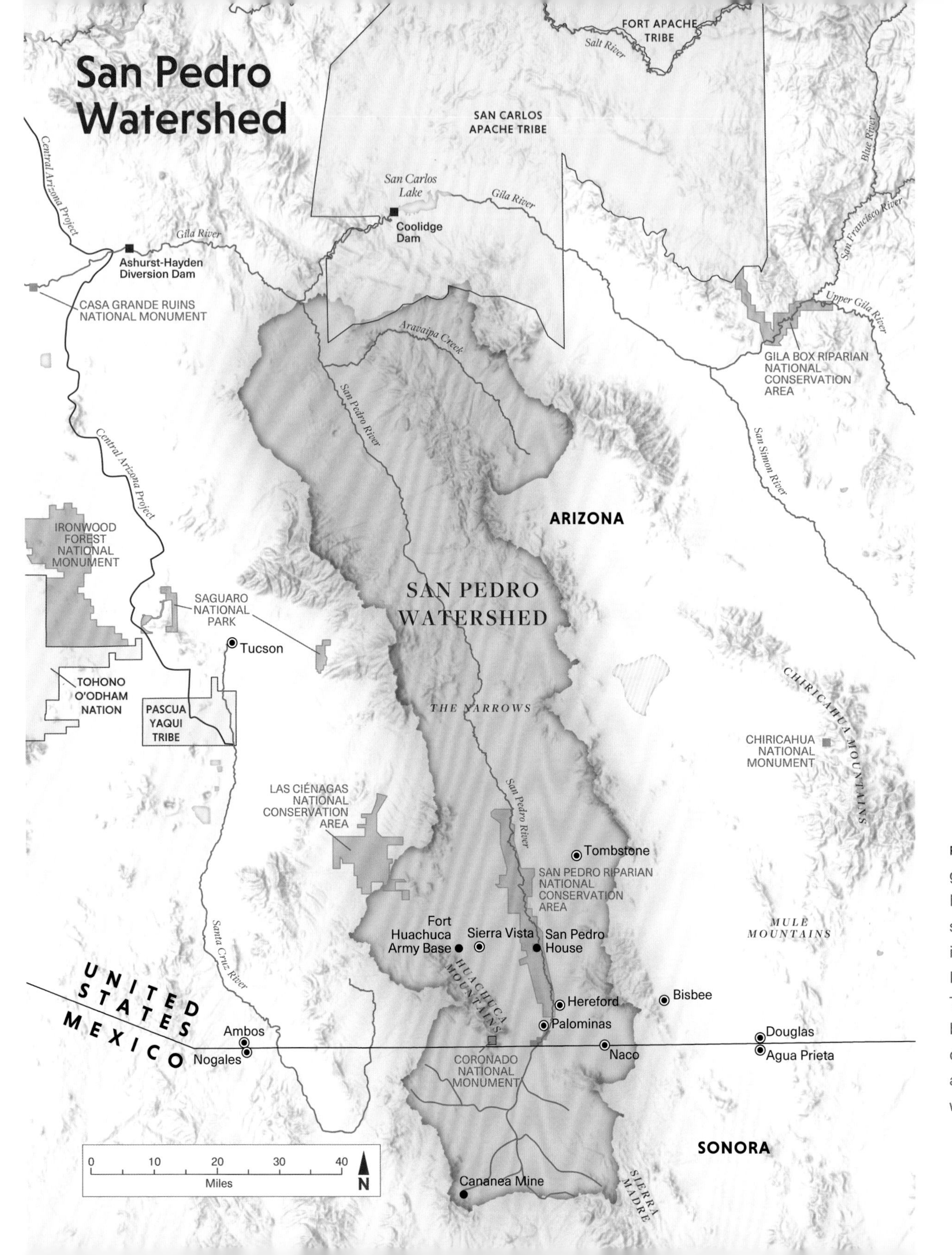

PAGE 146 Semidesert grassland atop Coronado Peak is draped in a golden sunset on the borderlands in Coronado National Monument, Arizona. The San Pedro River and border wall are in view on the upper left, Mexico and the San Pedro headwaters on the right.

The original groundwater pump, a windmill stands idle on ranch land in southeast Arizona. Much of rural Arizona allows unlimited groundwater pumping, drawing down aquifers and drying out private wells.

and cools, forming towering clouds that release powerful rains providing half the annual moisture for southern Arizona. Life-zone biomes of oak and pine woodlands ascend from desert scrub and sacaton grasslands, where the Madrean sky-island bioregion supports more than seven thousand species of plants and animals and more than half of North American bird species. Jaguar, ocelot, mountain lion, and bobcat find refuge in sky islands.

Several small streams flow north from Mexico's sky-island mountain ranges, including the San Jose and La Mariquita, to form the headwaters of the San Pedro River, just ten miles south of the US-Mexico border. The San Pedro, a tributary of the Gila River, and the Santa Cruz River, a mostly dry Gila River tributary that flows through Tucson, are the only two south-to-north-flowing international rivers in the Colorado River watershed. The San Pedro, with her intermittent flow and powerful flood regime, challenges us to reimagine all we know about rivers.

While photographing in the Huachuca Mountains one blustery December morning, I bumped into a Forest Service volunteer on the rough Miller Canyon road; rolling down his window, he asked what I was up to. "Photographing the San Pedro for a river story," I replied. To which he said, "It's a pissant river, except when it's not." As he drove away, I wondered if he knew that every life in the Sierra Vista valley below depends on the San Pedro. The "except when it's not" part was insightful, though; the little river becomes a raging torrent in monsoonal flash floods.

The city of Sierra Vista and Fort Huachuca Army Base anchor the San Pedro River Basin communities, a little over an hour southeast of Tucson. From the US-Mexico border, the river meanders through the San Pedro Riparian National Conservation Area, managed by the US Bureau of Land Management—and the nation's first RNCA, created to protect forty miles of the upper San Pedro River's lush riparian corridor for local and migrating wildlife. Flowing north between volcanic hills near Tombstone, Arizona, the San Pedro continues a 143-mile journey to its confluence with the Gila River in the town of Winkelman, Arizona; the last sixty miles of the San Pedro, with cottonwood-willow gallery forest and old-growth honey mesquite bosque woodlands, are designated the Lower San Pedro Important Bird Area.

STEPPING INTO THE RIVER CORRIDOR FROM THE ARID sacaton grasslands feels like a fantasy, a different world, where in a few steps from parched grass, the air is moist, the scent a stirred-up cycle of renewal and decay, a cathedral arch of cottonwoods overhead, and birdsong—symphonic, surround-sound birdsong filling the riparian air. The river you see is the top of the water table, spotty in places: dry at the surface and flowing underground in between wet areas, rippling in slow meanders elsewhere. It's best to test the saturated and boot-sucking quicksand when walking the riverbed, where you'll also see jumbled intertwined logs, branches, entire trees, and detritus, piled up against thick cottonwood trunks and oddly out of place—evidence of massive monsoon flash floods rearranging and remaking the floodplain from late July into August. The storms unleash an explosion of life-giving energy, revitalizing willow and cottonwood, while recharging the alluvial aquifer: groundwater that flows unseen beneath the riverbed.

With its south-to-north orientation, healthy riparian cottonwood-willow ecosystem, and flowing surface water, the San Pedro is a hemispherically important river system for migrating neotropical birds with winter ranges in Central and South America. Millions of birds rely on the San Pedro River corridor as a critical stopover site in spring and autumn, with 375 documented bird species using the riparian area as critical habitat in their life cycles. The San Pedro's cottonwood and willow host threatened yellow-billed cuckoos and endangered southwest willow flycatchers through summer. Holly Richter, Arizona Water Projects director for The Nature Conservancy, described tent caterpillars, a primary food source for the yellow-billed cuckoo, "dropping from cottonwoods like rain." The list goes on: 84 species of mammals, 14 species of fish, 41 species of reptiles and amphibians, all endemic to the San Pedro. All of this life, human as well as wild, depends on groundwater in balance with surface flows.

We often imagine groundwater as an underground lake, but groundwater beneath the surface of Southwest rivers—the alluvial aquifer—is more like a slow-moving sponge: water slowly seeping through massive layers of sand, gravel, clay, and stone forming a deep, porous layer. Sitting at a picnic table overlooking the floodplain east of Sierra Vista, Holly said, "You can't separate groundwater from surface water." About 40 percent of Arizona's water supply is pumped groundwater, which is finite. Forty years of continuous groundwater pumping, primarily for agriculture, has so imperiled the San Pedro that it simply can't recover on its own. Holly grabbed her car keys to make a point: "We could all get in our cars and leave this valley right now, and it wouldn't be enough to save this river."

Just one valley over to the west, the mostly dried-up Santa Cruz River offers a foreboding example of how unfettered groundwater pumping can decimate a river system. Groundwater use is heavily regulated in Phoenix and Tucson, and the 1980 Arizona Groundwater Management Act created active management areas and irrigation nonexpansion areas with limitations on groundwater usage, yet most of rural Arizona still allows unlimited groundwater pumping. Without human intervention for timely, continued groundwater recharge where it is needed most to keep a river flowing, Southwest rivers become sandy washes, unable to sustain life.

The Cochise Conservation and Recharge Network (CCRN) was formed in 2015 with partners City of Sierra Vista, Cochise County, Hereford Natural Resource Conservation District, and The Nature

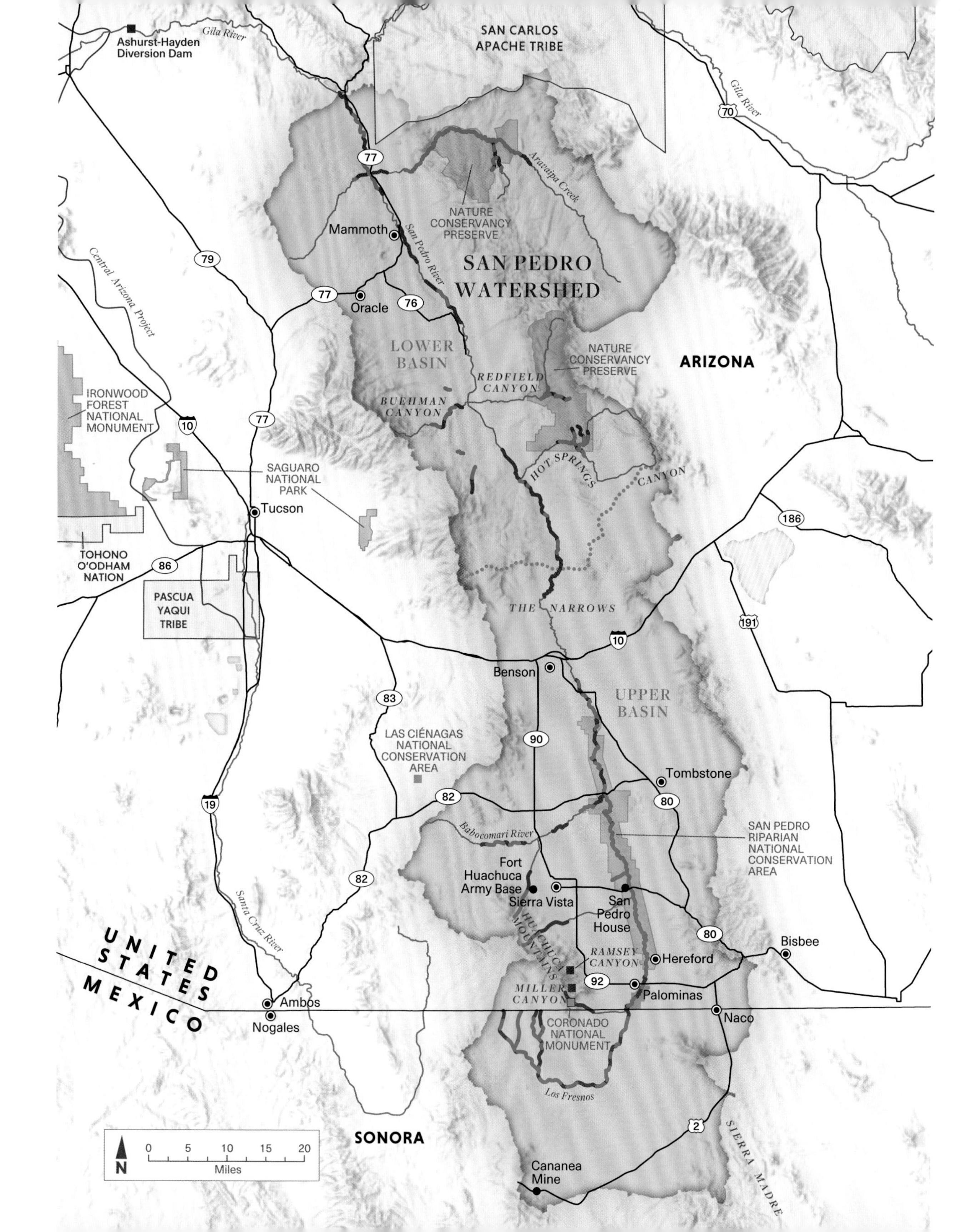

San Pedro River mapping of the extent of surface water in the watershed was conducted June 13–21, 2020, with blue indicating "wet" aboveground rivers and creeks and red indicating "dry" belowground rivers and creeks. (*Source:* "San Pedro River Surface Water Extent June 2020," The Nature Conservancy)

A Gila woodpecker with its brilliant red cap pauses on a cottonwood branch along the upper San Pedro River. These southwestern woodpeckers prefer desert scrub and grassland where cottonwoods or saguaro cactus provide nesting habitat.

Conservancy, joined later by the City of Bisbee and Fort Huachuca. The CCRN mission is "to implement a regional network of land- and water-management projects that result in a healthy watershed, flowing San Pedro River, conservation of water resources, and a vibrant local economy." The idea is to recharge the San Pedro River groundwater to "ensure the right amount of water is available in the right locations at the right times." There are eight recharge project sites in a twenty-five-mile stretch of the San Pedro where high-quality effluent or stormwater is infiltrated into the ground to stabilize and raise groundwater levels.

Holly Richter described US-Mexico transborder collaborations: "The Transboundary Aquifer Assessment Program was established in 2006 under a binational agreement to improve information about groundwater quality and quantity along the border for decision makers. . . . This program has been important . . . in both the San Pedro and Santa Cruz watersheds in Arizona." Holly, one of the founding members of the CCRN, explained that a volunteer effort to map wet and dry reaches of the San Pedro River has helped illustrate how groundwater and surface water interact: "In addition to binational cooperation through federal and state agencies, voluntary grassroots citizen-science programs have also reached across the border to create long-term data sets of great utility for managing water resources. The binational wet-dry mapping effort launched by The Nature Conservancy and BLM in 1999 on the San Pedro is an example."

Holly and I visited the Sierra Vista Environmental Operations Park site, where ducks swimming among tall cattails waving in the wind gave the impression of a high-desert wetland four miles uphill from the San Pedro floodplain. From here, effluent that's almost clean enough to drink migrates to the alluvial aquifer near the river, stabilizing surface flow.

Downhill by the river, birders and hikers gathered and dispersed at the San Pedro House, a local hub, to experience the wonders of the San Pedro on a network of hiking trails. Brawny cottonwoods surround the historical ranch house, restored by Friends of the San Pedro River, with bookstore and gift shop. The two biggest cottonwoods, aged between 90 and 130 years with massive trunks, had been dropping limbs lately, threatening the ranch house. While admiring one of the trees, a local birder pointed to tell me of a heart-shaped tree hole about thirty feet up where a locally known western screech owl is often seen. There was a calm here, visitors whispering and quietly noting the comings and goings of birds, the grounds well stocked with water, suet, and seed. I located a spot to settle in and witness Gila woodpeckers with red caps in a cottonwood, as white-crowned sparrows, the same bird seen on Colorado's high alpine

The slatted border wall leads to the San Pedro River where the river crosses the US-Mexico border. Much of Arizona's southern borderlands have been destroyed by border-wall construction and attendant roads and lights.

Prior to 2020, a simple barbed-wire fence (behind the crisscrossed fence) marked the international border in the San Pedro watershed, followed by this second fence that still enabled wildlife to move through the floodplain. In 2020 a new thirty-foot-tall bollard wall and a bridge with intensely bright lighting were built at the San Pedro River international border, making wildlife movement impossible in the wildlife-rich San Pedro River section of the borderlands.

tundra in summer, scratched for seed in thick brush. The screech owl stayed hidden from view that day.

FOR REASONS I DON'T FULLY UNDERSTAND—maybe because its creation is such a hostile act against fragile and beautiful imperiled lands—I was drawn to visit the border wall on my first San Pedro expedition, specifically where the San Pedro crosses the US-Mexico border. In the fall of 2019, the wall was going up at breakneck speed in Arizona on both private and public lands. All environmental laws, including the Endangered Species Act, Antiquities Act, and other legal protections, had been waived to add miles of wall in wild, remote, and relatively pristine border regions. To the west, Sonoran Desert lands sacred to the Tohono O'odham people had been bombed, bulldozed, and scraped—destroyed for more border wall.

I headed south and upstream from Sierra Vista, past Ramsey Canyon, then Miller Canyon, major cuts in the towering Huachuca Mountains, my directions pointing me to a right-hand turn just before Palominas, a mile or two from the border road. Making a number of rights and lefts, with border agents posted on each corner and dust billowing on bumpy roads, I drove past tidy ranchettes, eventually reaching a road bordering the San Pedro Riparian National Conservation Area, marked by a small sign and a strand of barbed wire lining sacaton grassland in the RNCA. Forewarned about ominous Keep Out signs, I continued through private lands ringed with American flags, with ample hand-painted warnings to anyone considering trespassing. The border wall appeared before me, its rusty slats standing tall, the Mexican grasslands looking more like wilderness than on the US side. A left-hand turn on a dusty, graded border road led slightly downhill to the San Pedro floodplain, where a glorious cottonwood gallery marks the river course and one of the most important wildlife migration corridors in the desert Southwest.

There was a small parking area above the river and a border agent watching the crossing from his white and green US Border Patrol truck. With camera and tripod, I nodded to the officer as I walked down to the floodplain, where the riverbed was cut by crisscrossed waist-high iron, with the taller slatted wall extending from either side of the river. Standing there transfixed, I studied the scene in suspended time. A handful of cows were loafing on the Mexican side, while tall cottonwoods, transitioning from green to autumn gold, waved on a warming breeze. No surface water was flowing in the dusty riverbed, as the San Pedro flowed in the alluvial aquifer deep beneath my feet.

Walking to the edge of the short riverbed fence, I thought that an ocelot, mountain lion, Mexican wolf, or jaguar could still cross here. Looking up toward the Huachuca Mountains, I could see where the wall ended

Coues (cooz) deer are an elfin white-tailed deer subspecies, standing about thirty inches tall at the shoulder, with proportionately larger ears than a whitetail's to help dissipate heat. Coues deer populate the sky islands of southeast Arizona, with this individual backed by a kaleidoscope of autumn color in The Nature Conservancy's Ramsey Canyon Preserve.

on a steep flank of the rugged range, giving rise to hopeful thoughts of wildlife moving through one small section of the borderlands. Turning away from the wall on the edge of grassland and riparian forest, I witnessed waist-high sacaton grasses bowing on the wind and cottonwood leaves quivering as they have for millennia; for a minute or two there was no conflict, no iron division, just beauty.

The Trump administration kept building border wall, exceeding 200 miles of wall across southern Arizona, destroying as much wild borderlands as possible before time ran out. In 2020 cottonwoods were removed at the San Pedro border crossing, and the riverbed's small iron fence was replaced with bollards spaced only three inches apart, plus a Border Patrol bridge and bright lights that disorient bats, owls, and songbirds, all of which migrate or hunt at night. Other than when gates over the river and watercourses along the wall are opened during explosive monsoon floods carrying entire trees and debris, there are no openings large enough for rabbit, desert tortoise, skunk, raccoon, coatimundi, opossum, coyote, Gila monster, badger, ringtail, black bear, javelina, ocelot, jaguar, or mountain lion to cross the international border.

Before the iron wall, there was just an ordinary barbed-wire fence demarcating the border. People and wildlife have migrated through this landscape for thousands of years, following the river in a historical succession of Indigenous Clovis people trailing mammoths 10,000 years ago, hunter-gatherer Cochise Culture between 2000 and 500 BC, then Mogollon, Hohokam, and Salado Cultures and the Sobaipuri people of the San Pedro before the arrival of the Spanish and Coronado in AD 1540. It is the land of Apache Chief Cochise and Geronimo, a medicine man of the Bedonkehe band of the Chiricahua Apache and leader in the Apache Wars, until thousands of US and Mexican soldiers captured the small remaining Chiricahua Apache band in 1886.

The arrival of the Southern Pacific Railroad to Arizona in 1881 brought the big cattle herds, overstocking the range first with cattle, followed by sheep, denuding the rich grasslands of cover and overrunning rivers, trampling, grazing, and drying out lush *ciénagas* (wetlands). While I don't aim to retrace the complex human history of the San Pedro, the river we have today is largely shaped by those events in the open range era, which ended with the Stock Raising Act of 1916, followed by the Taylor Grazing Act of 1934. The invention of the centrifugal pump in the 1940s, decades of unregulated groundwater pumping, and an extended human western migration are the drivers of today's groundwater crisis. Yet the San Pedro—the only undammed and free-flowing Southwest river—and the wildlife she supports still persevere.

The protected San Pedro River corridor, Huachuca Mountains, and surrounding grasslands make up some of the wildest country in the Southwest. If not for the border wall, the Apache Highlands would be largely contiguous for big animals to move through, and occasionally an endangered male jaguar or ocelot disperses from Mexico in search of a mate. A breeding population of 150 to 200 jaguars live about 130 miles south of the city of Douglas, Arizona, in Mexico's Sierra Madres, and the US Fish and Wildlife Service has designated critical habitat protection for jaguars in southern Arizona, in hopes that jaguars can establish a modest population in the United States. There is currently one known male jaguar in the Chiricahua Range about thirty miles east of the San Pedro and one endangered ocelot in the Huachuca Mountains. The odds are long for meaningful jaguar and ocelot conservation in the northernmost 1 percent of their range; yet if this habitat is wild enough for jaguar and ocelot, it's wild enough for mountain lion, black bear, and all of the enduring, endemic wildlife of the San Pedro watershed.

Leaving the border wall that autumn day, I ventured to The Nature Conservancy's Ramsey Canyon Preserve, where I hiked up into the Coronado National Forest through a kaleidoscope of red and gold in peak fall color. Atop a stone outcropping, I took in the view of Arizona pine forest, tracing a sinuous line of orange sycamore and bright red bigtooth maple marking the course of Ramsey Creek far below the overlook, where I imagined a mountain lion or jaguar moving unseen and on the hunt, flowing freely like water through an open landscape. Water. Life. Hope.

TOP Bigtooth maple leaves float on Ramsey Creek, blue sky overhead reflected in the stream flowing from the Huachuca Mountains into The Nature Conservancy's Ramsey Canyon Preserve in southeast Arizona.

BOTTOM The beauty of the San Pedro River cottonwood canopy near Palominas, Arizona, is reflected in surface water at the top of the water table. The pile of trees and debris on the right is a remnant of summer monsoon floods when the quiet San Pedro becomes a raging torrent. Human intervention—groundwater recharge—is necessary for surface water to continue flowing in the San Pedro, a still-wild river in south-east Arizona of critical importance for migrating birds in the northern hemisphere.

HOLLY RICHTER

"What I've learned is how unseen groundwater is for people and how important that is—that omission of the consideration of groundwater, frankly, for all rivers. Because what we value so highly is typically the surface water we can see, and this is human nature, but the lifeblood of much of that surface water is groundwater."

HORSE-RIDING RIVER CONSERVATIONIST HOLLY RICHTER lives and breathes the San Pedro. The river is just beyond her backyard, where tall cottonwoods reflect in the intermittent flow characteristic of the San Pedro. Holly earned her PhD studying the Yampa River in northwest Colorado, creating an ecological, hydrologic, geomorphic prediction model for the Yampa. Though that sounds complicated, Holly, who works for The Nature Conservancy as Arizona Water Projects director, thinks of herself as "a river conservationist who builds consensus on solutions." One of the founding members of both the Upper San Pedro Partnership—a consortium for protecting the San Pedro Riparian National Conservation Area (RNCA) and ensuring the long-term viability of Fort Huachuca—and the Cochise Conservation and Recharge Network, Holly has been instrumental in building partnerships and community since 1999.

From our first conversation, Holly stresses the important connection of groundwater to surface water and explains her own path to critically thinking about groundwater. "When I first arrived on the San Pedro," she tells me, "I had all kinds of questions, and those questions started with surface water, because people were telling me, 'Oh, the flows of the San Pedro are unchanged in the last hundred years,' and other people were saying, 'Oh, the flows of the San Pedro have changed so much; the river is dead.' Obviously the truth lay between those two bookends. But to get to the truth, we had to understand the river's connection today with groundwater. It was a long process to get there, frankly, to develop the tools that could not only let us see where we are at today, but where we'd like to go in the future as a community."

Holly describes the collaboration to save the San Pedro as "an incrementally slow process, like the accretion of groundwater itself." The collaborative learning process worked through legal, economic, and social issues to reach a common understanding of how water works above- and belowground, a learning experience that Holly calls "a major breakthrough." Understanding the relationship of surface water and groundwater is inherently challenging. "Because groundwater is so complex in the way that it moves through underground aquifers," says Holly, "and because we can't see it and we don't understand its movement and connection, it's commonly overlooked. So we see only part of the hydrologic cycle."

To monitor river health, in 1999 Holly began recruiting community volunteers to map the river on "the hottest day of the year," typically the third Saturday in June, before summer monsoon season. The beginning of the project, called wet-dry mapping, coincided

Holly Richter stands near her home under a canopy of cottonwood in the San Pedro River floodplain.

with the start of the current western megadrought and aridification in the San Pedro watershed. Holly describes the project: "People walk or ride horses along desert streams to map where the streams have water present and where they are dry. Creating this decades-long, uninterrupted data set is helping scientists and managers better understand and manage our riparian and aquatic habitats."

The project has grown from wet-dry mapping the San Pedro RNCA to mapping more than 280 miles of the river and its major tributaries in Mexico, plus the middle and lower reaches of the San Pedro, with partners on both sides of the border. Beyond quantifying river behavior over time, wet-dry mapping aids in understanding how groundwater and surface water interact, helps identify conservation needs and where to implement ecological research and monitoring, and contributes to managing fish and wildlife populations and their habitat. Wet-dry mapping now covers other rivers in Arizona and beyond, to monitor the extent of perennial surface flow in dryland rivers and streams.

Holly adds something special about the wet-dry mapping project: "I recruit a wide variety of volunteers from the community—students, businesspeople, Realtors, elected officials, councilmembers, landowners, conservationists, teachers . . . and scientists from the community to build consensus. Each team of volunteers had a diversity of perspectives but always came back from the river after mapping with identical observations about what was really happening with its flows. That was the coolest part—by doing this together, we're getting divergent views to become one." ✹

OPPOSITE Splashes of colorful sycamore, bigtooth maple, and cottonwood trees mark the watercourse of Ramsey Creek in The Nature Conservancy's Ramsey Canyon Preserve, where it tumbles from the Huachuca Mountains in the Apache Highlands ecoregion, Arizona.

RIGHT White-crowned sparrows can be spotted in all the major habitats of the Colorado River watershed, like this one in the San Pedro Riparian National Conservation Area, Arizona. It's a delight to witness flocks of these beautiful sparrows pecking seeds in desert shrub through winter and in gnarled krummholz trees and alpine tundra breeding habitat at the head of the watershed in summer.

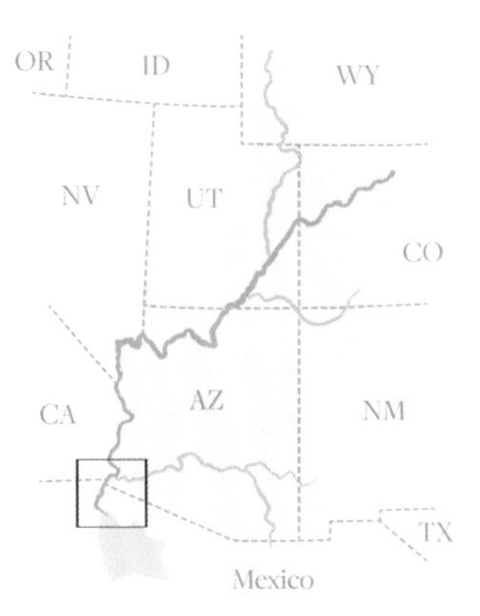

Chapter 7

GREENING THE DELTA

US-Mexico Collaboration

An Interview with Audubon's Jennifer Pitt

THE COLORADO RIVER DELTA IN MEXICO is often dismissed as dead, the main stem of the Colorado disappearing in desert sand just south of the US border, where the last of the mighty river is diverted from Morelos Dam to the Mexicali Valley. One of Mexico's most productive agricultural regions, the Mexicali Valley is contiguous with the Imperial Valley in Southern California. Although the Colorado River no longer reaches the Gulf of California, water is flowing seasonally in the Colorado River Delta as part of Minute 323, an international agreement that establishes how the United States and Mexico share Colorado River water to support a remarkable binational conservation restoration effort in Mexico. This water-shortage sharing agreement that is focused on sustainable use between the United States and Mexico states that Mexico can continue to store water in Lake Mead, and the United States supports water efficiency projects in Mexico that will save 200,000 acre-feet of water. Habitat restoration and scientific study are funded by both countries for a decade under the agreement.

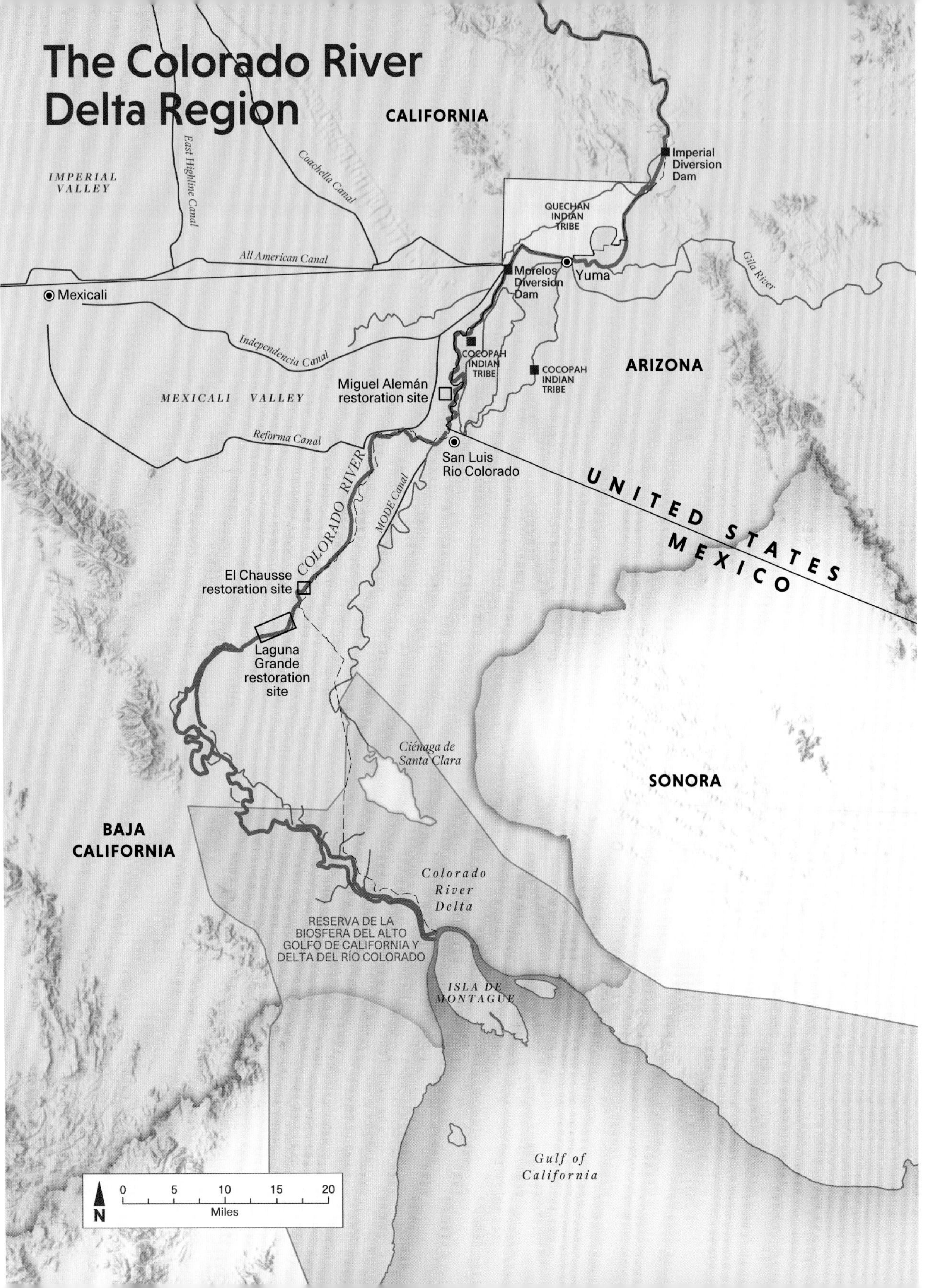

PAGE 162 Providing a modern glimpse into the "milk and honey wilderness" described by Aldo Leopold in 1922, the wetlands of Ciénaga de Santa Clara are critical habitat for migrating birds and other wildlife in the Colorado River Delta. In 1977, the United States began sending salty agricultural runoff unsuitable for agriculture to the Santa Clara Slough, creating an accidental and most important wetland in the Colorado River Delta, with 261 documented species of birds and 189 species of migrating birds. The wetland is home to 280,000 shorebirds and marsh birds—endangered Yuma clapper rails, Virginia rails, California black rails—and is a stopover site for 81 species of neotropical migrating birds. Binational collaboration is crucial to protecting the health of Ciénaga de Santa Clara in Mexico's upper Gulf of California and Colorado River Delta Biosphere Reserve. (LightHawk aerial support)

In the Law of the River, a "Minute" is an addendum to the US-Mexico Water Treaty of 1944, establishing how the two nations share Colorado River water. In 2017, Minute 323 replaced Minute 319, a broad approach including shortage sharing, binational investment in water conservation, water exchanges, authorization for Mexico to store water in Lake Mead, and binational commitments to restoration in the Delta—this last component enabling the much-celebrated 2014 "Pulse Flow" that reconnected the main stem of the Colorado River to the Gulf of California. This onetime event released 105,392 acre-feet of Colorado River water from Morelos Dam, delivered to the Colorado River Delta between March 23 and May 18, 2014. Morelos, the last dam on the Colorado, straddles the US-Mexico border between the states of Baja California and Arizona; maintained by Mexico, Morelos Dam allows Mexico to release its water allotment from the Colorado. While Lake Mead's primary job is to store water for the Lower Basin states (Nevada, Arizona, and California), storing Mexico's share in Lake Mead is intended to maintain healthy reservoir levels.

In spite of the dry river channel in the Delta and claims that the Colorado is a dying river, there is nuance in the Delta's story, from the Laguna Grande restoration site to Ciénaga de Santa Clara and Isla de Montague at the river's mouth. Nature is responding to habitat restoration, supporting some 18 million migrating birds of more than a hundred species moving through the Delta in spring.

Jennifer Pitt, Audubon's Colorado River Program director, has been engaged in and leading Colorado River Delta conservation efforts for more than two decades, well before the visionary idea of restoring riparian habitat where the Colorado once flowed to the sea. Drawn to Jennifer's decades of collaborative conservation and a promising message of resiliency and international collaboration, I had a conversation with her about the Delta, binational conservation, and signs of hope in restoration of the Colorado River Delta.

DS: YOU'VE BEEN WORKING ON COLORADO RIVER DELTA conservation for more than twenty years. Please talk about your background and what led you to the Delta.

JP: IF I THINK BACK, I DECIDED WHEN I WAS GETTING MY master's to focus on water because it touches everything. At the time I thought about it in a physical way, in terms of a holistic approach to landscapes. What I have come to appreciate since then is that water does touch everything. But my understanding has really evolved over time working on the Colorado River—it touches and is touched by politics and governance and policy and law and economics and culture and history and how we live in our communities. And it's interesting that water is all of that, because I think many people don't really perceive how central [water] is and how it runs through so much of our society.

Literally, I fell into work in the Delta because right after college I had worked as a park ranger at Mesa Verde [National Park], and I fell in love with the Rocky Mountains. I was working back East and trying to find my way back out to Colorado when I was fortunate enough to get hired by Environmental Defense Fund in the late nineties. They literally just needed to get a report completed and I was handed the Delta as an assignment. So I kind of bumped into it not knowing much initially. The more interesting question is, Why did I stick with it for all these years?

The Colorado River is an interesting river and people get bitten by the bug, they stick with it, and that goes for the Delta for sure. I have colleagues I've been working with this whole time. I think people stick with the Colorado River because it embodies complexity in terms of running through everything in a very storied way. It has an outsize place in history and it is an outsize place for the cultures of people who have been here since time immemorial.

On the US-Mexico international border, the Mexico allocation of the Colorado River is diverted west at Morelos Dam to Mexicali agricultural fields. In this frame, a trickle of water flows into the historical main channel of the Colorado River. The Mexican city of Algadones is in the lower right, with Yuma lettuce fields on the left (north of the border). Today, under Minute 323, a binational water-shortage sharing agreement between the United States and Mexico, a small amount of water is allocated to habitat restoration in the Colorado River Delta floodplain. (LightHawk aerial support)

DS: I'VE READ ALDO LEOPOLD'S ACCOUNT OF the Delta from his 1922 expedition, ironically the year of the Colorado River Compact. For reference and relative ecological importance, can you paint a picture of the Delta before dams, diversions, and settlement?

JP: LEOPOLD DEFINITELY HIT THE JACKPOT with that visit in 1922. He described a "milk and honey wilderness" created by the meandering Colorado River. The river was "everywhere and nowhere," and he described the sky almost blackened from the hordes of birds, egrets, and cormorants . . . at times the birds were so abundant, they looked like a snowstorm. He provided us with a very colorful record. To the best of our knowledge, the ecosystem covered about a million and a half acres in extent.

The whole river was flowing unobstructed to its delta, so in snowmelt season, late spring or early summer, it would expand. You can actually see that footprint of the big wide river from satellite photos or by flying over it. Later in the year, by September, October, it would retreat to its base flow, but that was still enormous. While the common conception of the Colorado River is based on its origins in the Rocky Mountains or the Grand Canyon, which was carved with its immense force, most people don't realize that the Delta is a vast floodplain created when the river deposited all that eroded rock from the Grand Canyon, spread out over the landscape. When the river flowed there, it was a vast, flat, watery, and biologically productive place.

DS: WHAT WERE THE CONDITIONS ECOLOGICALLY AND politically in the late nineties when you began working in the Delta?

JP: CERTAINLY WHEN IT CAME TO THE UNITED STATES and Mexico and their relationship on the Colorado River, they were clearly treating each other at arm's length. The US-Mexico Water Treaty, which dates back to 1944, seemed functional enough from the perspective of water managers who were concerned with ensuring delivery to water users, taking water off the river and putting it to economic use. With one exception—an agreement [1974 Colorado River Basin Salinity Control Act] regulating the salinity of the Colorado River water that the United States can send to Mexico, negotiated through the sixties and early seventies to address a dispute over water quality—there really hadn't been any updates to the treaty.

And while the two countries use the US and Mexican sections of the International Boundary and Water Commission [established in 1889 and expanded in the 1944 treaty] to manage their binational relationship over the river, those two sections were maintaining physical infrastructure and really looking at treaty implementation with an engineering perspective and not much else. I remember thinking in the early days about the problem of the desiccated Delta: how are we going to convince either of these countries to take hold of the issue and do something about it? The United States looked at the Delta and figured it was in another country, not their problem. When Mexico looked at their sandblasted landscape, they didn't think they could do anything about it; they had no control over the water because all of the dams were in the United States.

One of the things that really compelled the conservation community at that time was the work of a lovely man, Dr. Ed Glenn, a professor at the University of Arizona for many years who had gone down to the Delta. He was actually an environmental science professor, in the biological sciences, and his life's work up until that point had been dedicated to finding ways to improve human nutrition in Africa by looking at what plants would grow in brackish water. He was going on some exploratory trips down into Mexico to look at saline ecosystems, to see what plants were growing in saltier waters, to see what might grow on parts of the African continent where there were nutrition and/or or hunger concerns. He started noticing pockets of native habitat and documenting them.

Dr. Glenn published in the 1990s, pointing out that because of return flows from agriculture uses of water in the footprints of the Colorado River Delta, and also because of some occasional spills—remember that in the eighties and nineties the reservoirs were full, and in big water years there were occasionally flood releases—these flows were actually regenerating the native floodplain forest, cottonwoods and willows, those trees that are all-too-often missing from our rivers in the southwestern corner of the United States. He actually quantified that there was more native habitat on the Colorado River between the border and the Gulf [of California] than there was between Hoover Dam and the border—maybe on the order of ten times more in the 1990s. We took notice of that in the fact that the river wasn't really flowing and started to think about what you could do with a very modest amount of water and some proactive management. And that's really what inspired us, but also reflects what the conditions were.

DS: WHY ARE THE TWO BINATIONAL water-shortage sharing agreements, Minutes 319 and 323, important, especially in a prolonged megadrought?

JP: THOSE AGREEMENTS ARE CRITICAL. It's worth pointing out that in August 2021, the US Secretary of the Interior for the first time ever declared a shortage on the Colorado River—reducing deliveries to the Lower Basin states of Arizona and Nevada [California wasn't affected yet], and according to the terms of Minute 323, Mexico took a shortage as well. The United States imposed a Colorado River water shortage on Mexico without a hiccup. There was no drama. You can look at those agreements as a piece of paper; you can also think of them as the embodiment of relationship building and trust. The two countries signed them voluntarily, not because a court ordered them to and not because anyone held a gun to their heads, but because Minute 323 is an agreement they believe is in the best interest of both sovereign nations. That is what allowed the reduction to be implemented so smoothly.

In the process of negotiating those agreements, Mexico was in no way required to sign up and say "We will voluntarily agree to take a shortage," particularly when there are plenty of people who will point out from the Mexican side of the border that the Colorado River sure looks like an overallocated water supply. Mexico's federal negotiators, in order to sign the agreement, had to negotiate terms that were a net positive for Mexico. To be fair, if there was no agreement, the upstream nation usually is the one that controls the water supply and what happens to the river flowing downstream. So there were some risks for Mexico. But there are considerable benefits that Mexico was able to negotiate for in that agreement, which allowed them to agree to the shortage provisions, and that includes the provisions to restore habitat in the Colorado River Delta.

The other big component of the agreement was the US investment in helping Mexico upgrade irrigation infrastructure in the Mexicali Valley, which they have implemented and are continuing to implement—and need desperately as climate change reduces the Colorado River supply much faster than most people expected. All water users are going to have to figure out how to use less water. Those investments the United States is providing are allowing Mexico to do things like install telemetry that enables better management of their water, funding to line canals and to fix canals that were damaged by earthquakes. That is also enormously important.

DS: THE 2014 PULSE FLOW SAW THE COLORADO river reach the Gulf of California for the first time in decades. It seems like a long time ago, yet it left a big imprint on folks. Why does the 2014 Pulse Flow matter so much?

JP: IN PART IT GOES BACK TO OUR UNDERstanding of what's been so broken about the Colorado River Delta—the Pulse Flow was meaningful because it created a river where one had been missing for decades. But I also think people saw the Pulse Flow and understood that the United States and Mexico were doing something good together, in a way that was perhaps unexpected at the time. That was novel. I paid

Diverted Colorado River water flows into El Chausse restoration site in the state of Baja California, Mexico. With less than 1 percent of historical flows redirected to restoration in the Colorado River Delta, Pronatura Noroeste and conservation partners in the Raise the River Alliance are returning life to the Delta. The site is stunning, with dense native cottonwood, willow, and other replanted native vegetation as well as beaver and birdlife repopulating this living riparian landscape.

TOP Cottonwood, willow, sweet mesquite, several varieties of palo verde, frutillo bush, cenizo brush, and more native plant species such as those growing in this greenhouse have been restored by Pronatura Noroeste to the 469-acre Miguel Alemán restoration site. Bird species diversity on the restored site has increased dramatically from 2010 when 23 bird species were documented to 123 species eleven years after the restoration.

BOTTOM Dilan Ortiz and Marylu Sandoval of Mexican conservation group Pronatura Noroeste display cottonwood and willow plants, cultivated in the greenhouse where native Delta riparian vegetation is grown on the Miguel Alemán restoration site.

attention to the amount of media coverage of the Pulse Flow, which was unprecedented.

There were stories around the globe, because there were people who love rivers and are nature lovers who were seeing it as a sign of something hopeful and positive, as a sign that even in the twenty-first century, humanity can do good when they set their minds to it. The Pulse Flow was also widely reported and celebrated throughout the Colorado River Basin. In that context, it was particularly important for all the people who have a hand in Colorado River management to know that the entire decentralized governance system of the Colorado River had agreed to and supported the Pulse Flow. Many people involved in Colorado River management, people I would not have identified as environmental advocates, commented that they were proud of this outcome.

Another way to understand what the Pulse Flow meant for people is locally, in terms of the reaction in the communities who live right on top of that mostly dry riverbed. More than one million Mexicali Valley residents live amid catastrophic environmental degradation. It certainly has struck me that if you live in the Mexican city of San Luis Rio Colorado, your hometown is named after the Colorado River, but you live next to a dry, sandy channel. You have to drive over a toll bridge to get in and out of town, but the bridge goes over sand. It's kind of stunning.

Locals really celebrated the return of the river. The community organized a huge cleanup to make sure that when the water started running, it didn't carry a raft of trash. I spent weeks in the Delta during the Pulse Flow and many times observed older people coming up to the river and kneeling down and putting their hands in it, almost like greeting someone or something that they hadn't seen in a long time. And I also saw a lot of those same older folks bringing young kids, perhaps their grandkids, to see a river that they had probably never seen before. It became an incredible community event, basically an eight-week spontaneous river fiesta that emerged on the banks of the Colorado River in the Delta.

DS: WHAT IS THE SCALE OF RESTORATION AND BENEFIT to birds relative to the amount of water used for conservation in these times of climate-driven megadrought?

JP: I THINK IT IS NECESSARY TO POINT OUT THAT THE amount of water being used for restoration is far less than 1 percent of the river's historic average annual flow. It's a tiny, tiny amount of water in relative terms. My NGO [nongovernmental organization] colleagues in Mexico—the Sonoran Institute, Pronatura Noroeste, and Restauremos el Colorado—have painstakingly hand-built more than a thousand acres of native floodplain habitat [at the Laguna Grande, El Chausse, and Miguel Alemán restoration sites] that are now lush with cottonwoods and willows and mesquite and other native understory plants.

When you walk into a restored cottonwood grove, particularly the ones that have been standing now for a decade, you walk into a transformed place. The temperature is different, the light is different, it smells different, the air feels different, it feels moist—you're standing on leaf litter. It is just so transformational. Relative to that missing million-and-a-half-acre ecosystem, a thousand restored acres is tiny, but it is located on the river corridor and is helping to reestablish connectivity for the river, for the animals that depend on that habitat. Under the terms of the Minutes, there is robust monitoring that involves not only the two federal governments but also universities from both sides of the border and NGOs as well. The birds, in particular, have responded to this new habitat and to water flowing in the Delta. In response to the 2014 Pulse Flow, bird species diversity increased 42 percent and bird abundance increased 20 percent.

DS: WHAT DOES SEEING THE RESTORATION and flow feel like to you personally?

JP: I CERTAINLY HAD TO PUT IN AN ENORMOUS amount of time in conference rooms and symposium halls talking about the Colorado River before I saw anything change. I wrote reports and published articles in law journals, science journals, policy journals. It could feel a little abstract and intangible. Seeing something that was an idea get turned into a flowing river, trees creating shade, birds singing, boats on a river, repairing even just a little bit of the devastation wrought on the Delta, that has been incredibly empowering for me and my colleagues. I revel in the fact that it's actually real.

DS: YOU WORK CLOSELY WITH DEDICATED Mexican conservation groups and individuals. Please tell us about these partners and wonderful people.

JP: ONE OF THE GREAT FORTUNES OF MY LIFE is that the trajectory of my career has been a path that I've traveled with people that I met back in the late nineties and I still work with. I think all of us were compelled by the same things—the nature of the problem, and then our early indications that we were making some progress. Once we had some success, it really became almost impossible to walk away because it's just rare that you get to work on something that has this kind of forward momentum and success. Today [our coalition is] known as the Raise the River Alliance, which includes Audubon Society, The Nature Conservancy, Pronatura Noroeste, Sonoran Institute, the Redford Center, and Restauremos el Colorado.

An aerial perspective of the El Chausse restoration site in Mexico's Colorado River floodplain shows the verdant green of restored wetland where invasive salt cedar and other nonnative plants were dominant with the absence of water. The remarkable recovery of Delta restoration sites is made possible with hard work and a small amount of Colorado River water diverted for restoration. (LightHawk aerial support)

One person who must be mentioned is Osvel Hinojosa-Huerta. Osvel is a birder at heart. I met him when he was getting his PhD at the University of Arizona. Although he's moved on to the Cornell Ornithological Labs, I remember he said to me, "Jennifer, you sit in the meetings and talk about water; I'm just going to go look at the birds." And over time, he started sitting in the meetings and talking about water with me, and he definitely was one of my main partners in working through what we had to do to gain trust and understanding from water managers at local, state, and federal levels—he in Mexico and me in the United States—and to have them understand that we were not trying to dismantle the entire infrastructure system and rule of law on the Colorado River. We really were just trying to do something about the Delta.

Another person who's very important to this story is Peter Culp. He's an attorney who now has his own firm. I met him when he was in law school; he wrote an award-winning paper on Colorado River policy and that it would take a new Minute between the two countries to start to restore the Delta. And he really is a genius at understanding negotiations and how to look at different interests in a multiplayer, multifaceted negotiation context. He really helped us see our way through what we used to call three-dimensional chess.

Francisco Zamora, who works with the Sonoran Institute, was hired by the institute right out of his PhD program, maybe back in 2000 or 2001. He really built up their program, and I think part of his genius—he has not been as involved in the water negotiations part of things, but he just got a spark in his eye and a vision for what restoration could look like. He started experimenting with, What could you actually do in that delta? He got trees planted and watered before we had a binational agreement, and that little bit of native habitat that he got to thrive on the ground was really instrumental as we started to take some of our federal leadership and state leadership to see the Delta, to be able to point to as an example of what we want to do. Then they had that tangible example of what we were aiming for.

One more person I want to mention is Yamillet Carrillo. I met her when she was right out of her undergrad, and then she went back and got her master's, then her PhD, at the University of Arizona. She got very interested in water management at the local level and the culture that was built around water management in the Mexicali Valley. She, with our coalition of NGOs, established our Colorado River Delta Water Trust, which is still operating today. That is part of how we deliver water resources to these created native habitats that we're developing. She did unprecedented work in the Mexicali Valley and built an institution that is still central to our restoration efforts today.

So that's not everybody, but the key people I thought of from the beginning who are part of this story as well. There are others, many others, who have joined the effort since those early days, but these are the people who were there at the beginning and stuck around to see it through.

DS: **IS LONG-TERM RESILIENCE POSSIBLE FOR THE DELTA?** And what gives you hope in a warming world?

JP: **I AM DEEPLY WORRIED, YET I FEEL LIKE THE LESSON** I learned from the last two decades of work is that when the governments signed the Minutes, they were adopting policy that reflects what society values. As climate change drives water scarcity, we are going to again and again confront the fact that there's not enough water for everything that we have been accustomed to using water for. Historically, when the laws and policy were established for using Colorado River water, people assumed that they understood the volume of the water supply and that it was renewable. Today it is clear those assumptions were not correct. Climate change is aridifying the Colorado River Basin. Already the average volume of the river's water supply in the twenty-first century is 20 percent reduced from the twentieth-century supply. Colorado River water supply and demand are out of balance. We know that because there isn't any

TOP The Janitzio restoration site is dominated by invasive vegetation and garbage typical of each Delta site before restoration work begins. Heavy equipment will remove the invasive vegetation prior to replanting and returning flowing Colorado River water to the site.

BOTTOM Stepping from desert scrubland into the riparian floodplain of the Miguel Alemán restoration site is a full sensory experience, with the crunch of leaf litter, scent of loam and new growth, moist air, and cool of shade from the blistering summer sun. To visit a Delta restoration site is to reimagine the possible, a return of riparian life and hope in flow and human empathy for the river. Recovery can be measured in wildlife biodiversity—Marylu Sandoval explained that prior to restoration, 23 bird species were documented at this site; once the restoration matured, 123 bird species were documented, a fivefold increase!

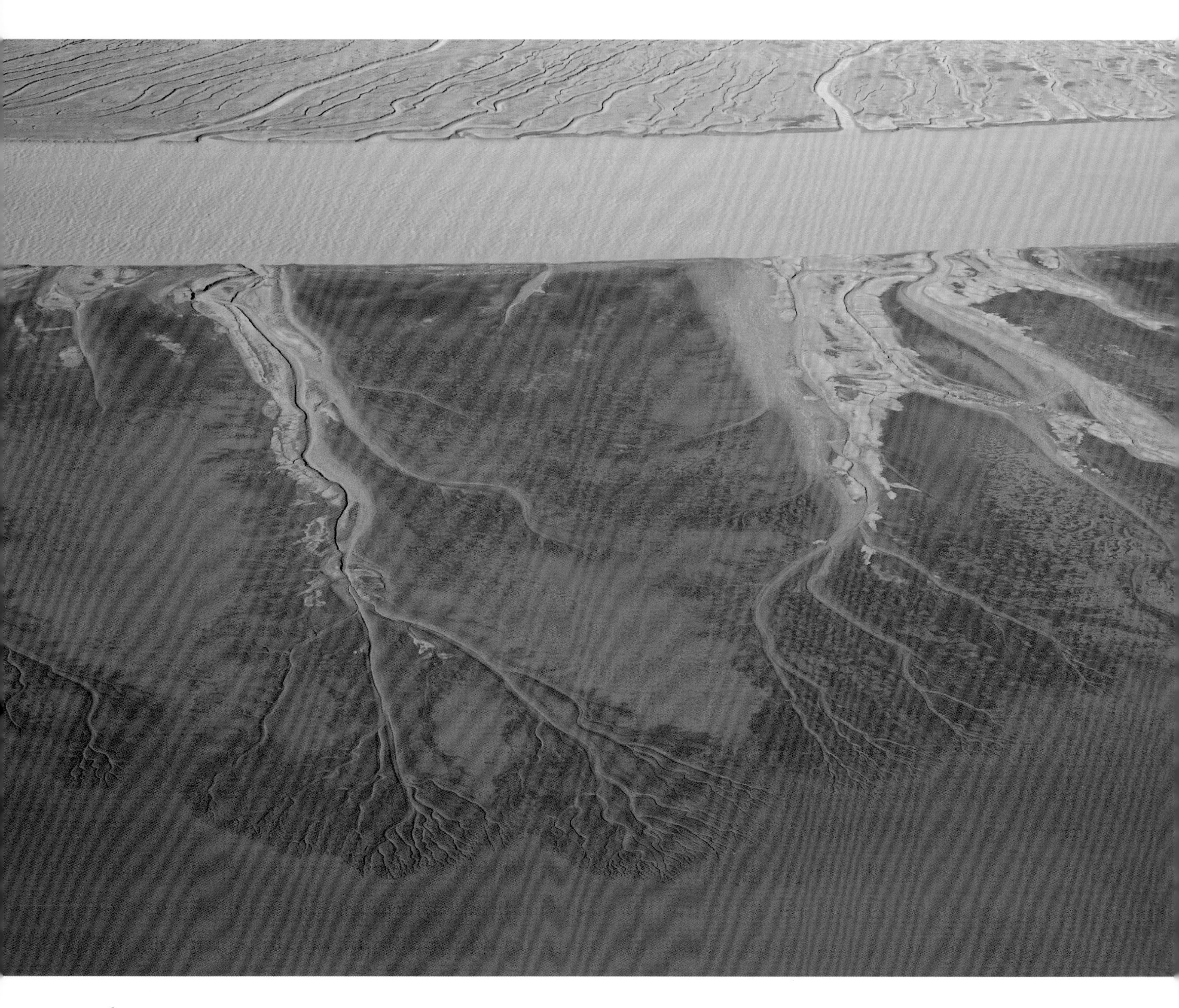

water flowing out the downstream end of the river, and we know that because the river's huge reservoirs are more empty than full.

The people engaged in managing the Colorado River—federal and state leaders from both countries, tribes, water-rights holders, environmental stakeholders—all of us need to be deliberate in thinking about what has value, what we want the Colorado's water to sustain. With climate change impacts upon us, relying on nineteenth-century law and twentieth-century infrastructure is not going to result in thriving communities, economies, cultural and natural resources that serve all of us in the basin.

Colorado River managers are going to have to make choices. I hope they will make them deliberately, rather than ceding to the status quo. We need management that avoids severe shortages in the communities least able to weather them and that addresses the needs of tribal communities that are not yet able to realize benefits from their water rights. We need management that sustains the fish and wildlife that depend on the creeks and rivers of the Colorado River Basin. State legislature interest in water right now, I'd say, is high.

I have faith in our society, that as we are asked to make choices we will manage water resources for what we value as a society, and that nature is one of those values. Yes, people need to eat, and farmers need water to grow our food. Yes, I want water to come out of my kitchen faucet. We all do. But I think we also all want a healthy natural world around us. Climate change is bringing unbelievable problems upon us. But if there is a silver lining, it may be that its impacts in the Colorado River Basin will force us to rethink these legal and infrastructure systems that have not necessarily served us well. Climate change is a disrupter and as we marshal the resources to adapt, we have an opportunity, an obligation even, to be thoughtful about what we will leave for the generations that follow us.

OPPOSITE Tidal waters form remarkable patterns in Delta sand at the river mouth and a tidal channel gives the hopeful impression of the Colorado River flowing to the Gulf of California. Although the Colorado River no longer flows to the sea, restoration work in the Delta has returned hope in human spirit and wild remnants reinvigorating some of the Colorado River Delta, once one of the most biodiverse places on earth. (LightHawk aerial support)

RIGHT Jennifer Pitt along Boulder Creek on the Colorado Front Range

---

JENNIFER PITT serves as Colorado River Program director for Audubon, where she works to protect and restore rivers throughout the Colorado River Basin. She serves as the US cochair of the binational work group whose partners will, through 2026, implement existing treaty commitments to environmental flows and habitat creation in the Colorado River Delta. Jennifer graduated from Harvard University and received a master's in environmental science and policy from the Yale School of Forestry and Environmental Studies. She is honored to earn a living advocating for a better life for birds and vulnerable communities and privileged to make her home in the shadow of the Rocky Mountains, where she is fairly successful at hiking her local mountain daily.

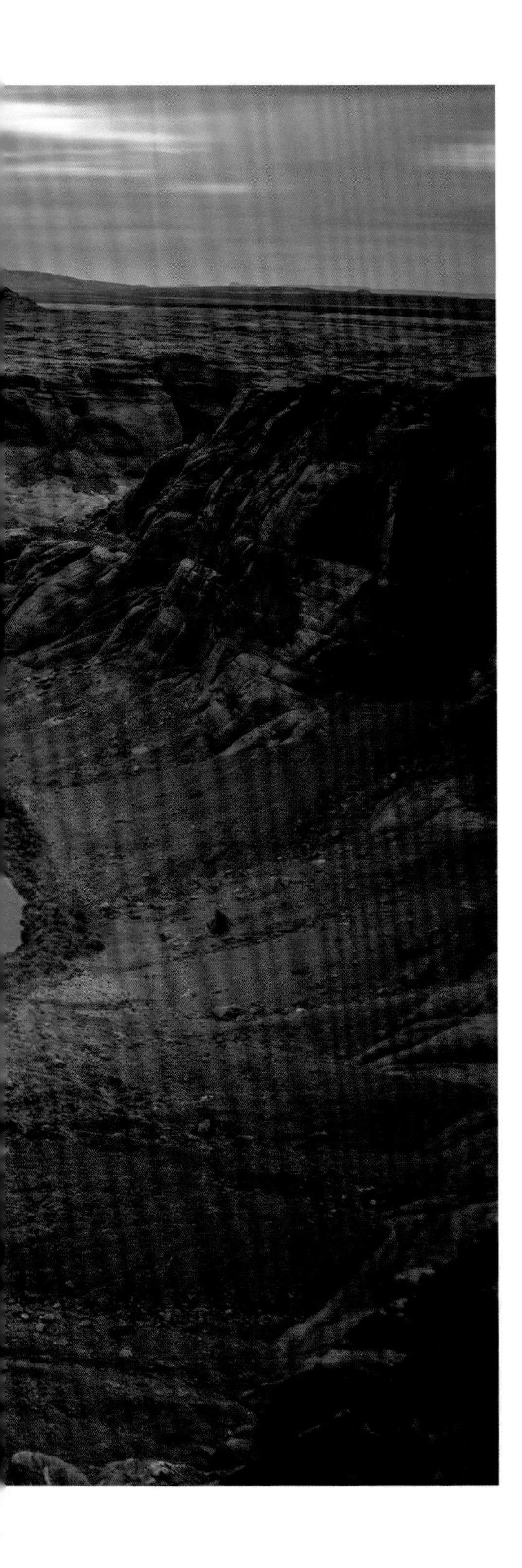

CONFLUENCE

The Colorado's Next Hundred Years

AS I WRITE THESE WORDS on the first of April, life is stirring throughout the watershed of the Colorado. Snowpack in the high mountains is at or near peak depth for the season. As tens of millions of birds migrate north, following river courses to reach summer breeding range, the big game animals—elk and mule deer (including the Kaibab Plateau herd of more than ten thousand mule deer on the Grand Canyon's North Rim)—are also browsing and using stopover sites to fuel up on their journeys to higher-elevation breeding grounds. Desert bighorn sheep are lambing in the deep canyons of the Colorado Plateau. Greater and Gunnison sage-grouse are displaying spectacularly on leks they've used for millennia, with mated hens retreating to set up nests tucked under sagebrush. Peregrine and prairie falcons are pairing up to lay eggs on a scrape high on a cliff aerie. Sandhill cranes are arriving on the Yampa River in northwest Colorado and the upper Green River tumbling from Wyoming's Wind River Range.

Throughout the watershed, farmers and ranchers are prepping for growing season, looking to the high peaks for hope when the Rockies release their frozen stockpile, the runoff peaking around Memorial Day. Humans are fanning out into open country and running swelling rivers as days lengthen and warm. In a way, we migrate too, seeking the season's renewal while steadily moving up from desert canyons in spring to tributary rivers and alpine tundra on summer adventures as snowpack recedes. Throughout the Colorado watershed, every living thing is in motion, on schedule and choreographed to longer days and spring runoff.

Snowpack in the Rocky Mountain headwaters has been decreasing in the second half of each winter for more than two decades (the wet, cold spring of 2011 excepted), a trend through the global heating-driven megadrought that can only be remedied by a lengthy break in the drought cycle and by more snow—preferably wet, deep, and cold enough to last well into spring. In 2022 scientists from UCLA and Columbia University reported that the current megadrought is the driest period in the American Southwest in the last twelve hundred years. The two big storage reservoirs on the Colorado River—Lakes Powell and Mead—have dropped to alarming lows over the last two decades, with Powell's ability to generate electricity now threatened. A new water-sharing agreement called the "500-Plus Plan," enacted in 2022 between the Lower Basin states of Nevada, Arizona, and California, requires the states to take cuts totaling 500,000 acre-feet in 2022 and 2023, raising water levels in Lake Mead. A total of $200 million from the states and federal government is also allocated to fund water efficiency projects.

Warnings of acute, systemic water shortage in the Colorado River system have come and gone with each spring runoff for decades—Lake Mead hasn't been full since 1983. The moment we were warned about is here. We can no longer bank on imaginary water any more than we can squeeze water from stone. Yet birds will migrate and spring life will explode in the watershed. This six-million-year-old river of ancient rhythms has resilience, renewal, and life inextricably tethered to her flow from mountain snowpack.

More than one hundred years into the 1922 Colorado River Compact, is it possible to reliably deliver water to forty million people, power cities, and provide water for agriculture and recreation? Do we have the collective courage to give rivers a voice by maintaining and living in balance with wildlife and natural systems, by protecting and restoring critical habitats, environmental flows, and wetland health? Even if there were a ready answer, it's a dynamic watershed undergoing extreme stress that is most visible and visceral in wildfire, and no one can predict how low future river flows will be.

The 1922 Compact was drafted when the combined populations of Los Angeles, Denver, Phoenix, and Las Vegas totaled fewer than one million people. All of the diminishing river flow and climate change impacts, nearly all of the growth and development of the West and the attendant destruction of wildlife habitats, have come in just a hundred years. Although no one in 1922 could have foreseen forty million people dependent on the Colorado, hubris and disregard of science and available flows have led us to this moment. A century of unbridled growth, a delayed awakening to a flawed "use it or lose it" mindset, a system that requires predetermined water delivery amounts to Lower Basin states rather than calibrating to the river we have, and the notion that the water will come from "somewhere" all contribute to our water reckoning in the West.

That reckoning begins with each of us asking, Where does my water come from? There is humility in acknowledging the limits of annual snowpack potential to sustain all life, in knowing that technology, however advanced, won't somehow fix our systemic water shortage. It's humbling to know that nature and rivers are still in charge—that for everyone in the Colorado's

Hoover Dam's concrete face and 395-foot-tall intake towers were exposed as Lake Mead, the nation's largest reservoir, shrank to 27 percent capacity in the summer of 2022.

PAGE 178 Downstream from Glen Canyon Dam and Page, Arizona, the Colorado River carved Horseshoe Bend, an incised meander in Glen Canyon National Recreation Area where the river turns back on itself.

OPPOSITE The Colorado River is impounded behind Glen Canyon Dam (lower left) in Lake Powell, the reservoir for water sent downstream to Lake Mead from the Upper Basin. Lake Powell's water level has steadily dropped since it was last full in 1983, visual evidence of the megadrought and shrinking snowpacks in the American West. The San Juan River's confluence at Lake Powell is just north of Page, Arizona (lower right). (LightHawk aerial support)

NEXT PAGES Hope in monsoon rainbows: after cold, heavy rains dumped on Black Canyon of the Gunnison National Park in Colorado, a double rainbow appeared over the Painted Wall, seen from a south-rim overlook. After the Gunnison River leaves Black Canyon, it flows through the Gunnison Gorge National Conservation Area and agricultural lands to its confluence with the Colorado River in the city of Grand Junction, Colorado.

watershed, all of our western lives, burgeoning cities, and economies are built on Colorado River current.

In 2026 there will be renegotiated operating guidelines for the Colorado River Compact, recalibrating to our water reality in the face of climate change—simply the river we have, with no buffer for systemic annual shortages, no bias for historically wetter periods to puff up the science. The grace of the 1922 Compact is a baked-in collaboration of the seven Colorado River Basin states and Mexico, and we go into this new water century hopeful as major cities and the big agricultural users are reducing water consumption. We waited way too long, but our way forward is through science, conservation, demand management, and education. A significant shortcoming in the 1922 Compact is allocation by fixed acre-feet to Lower Basin states, locking the entire watershed into systemic shortages rather than percentages of the river we have each year. The 2021 Declaration of Shortage on the Colorado River triggered a number of cuts to junior water rights. In times of shortage, those with senior, or "prior," water rights have stronger water rights than those with junior rights. Going forward, establishing triggers to recalibrate allocation based on actual water in the system is analogous to balancing our own checking accounts to prevent "overdraft" calamities that further stress the system.

What if the river drops to 11 million acre-feet (maf)? Or 10? Water consumption in the Upper Basin states (Colorado, Wyoming, Utah, and New Mexico) is stable at roughly 4 to 4.5 maf annually (having never used their full allocation of 7.5 maf), and the growing consensus is that the number needs to remain at 4.5 maf in order to stabilize the system. The idea doesn't mean Upper Basin states can't grow, but growth has to be smarter, and major cities have shown that water consumption can be reduced, even in periods of significant growth. Denver, for example, has reduced consumption to 1970s levels while growing rapidly. It doesn't make good sense to propose more reservoirs and pipelines when there isn't enough water to fill the remarkable capacity constructed in the glory years of dam building. The only variable in our control is demand, and water security must come from conservation and shared reductions described succinctly by Eric Kuhn and Lael Gilbert in the June 2021 issue of *Colorado Water* about climate change and adaptation, published by the Colorado Water Center at Colorado State University: "The only effective approach for the Upper Basin is to manage consumptive use demands at today's levels or less while simultaneously seeking an agreement with the Lower Basin where both basins share the burden of climate change."

Stepping into this next water century, the United States must honor its commitments to tribal nations and ensure universal access to clean water for Indigenous people to thrive. Our watershed community is not whole until everyone has access to clean water.

Beyond the mechanics of ensuring the delivery of water to every tap and "straw" in the river, beyond growth and development, even in the most arid landscapes in North America, the Colorado River watershed needs more people to know the river and her tributaries, more river keepers who know where our water comes from, a sense of our place in this magnificent watershed. I often wonder how long we'll go on installing and watering so much Kentucky bluegrass where shortgrass prairie, Colorado Plateau pinyon-juniper, and Sonoran sacaton grassland once were deep-rooted and self-sustaining.

Las Vegas has banned installation of turf and water waste associated with lawn irrigation and has mandated lawn removal—and replaces lawns for its residents. Why not in Denver, Saint George, Salt Lake City, all the major metro areas?

THE NARRATIVE OF A DYING COLORADO RIVER SUGGESTS that somehow the river is failing us and all of our dreams. In fact, it has taken just a few decades of overallocation and global heating to completely alter the hydrology of the American West. The hard work ahead requires widespread engagement in our water future, acknowledgment that we're all downstream neighbors with a fundamental right to clean-water access, and a shared mission of changing our relationship to water in the Colorado River watershed. The river is not dying; she flows with the same pure purpose and knowledge of six million years, long before Europeans colonized the West.

With no silver bullets to neatly solve our acute water shortage, water managers are grappling with only difficult choices of how to equitably share deep cuts to water usage across the watershed. Most of us won't be involved in the big decisions of renegotiated allocations and cuts. But there are forty million of us who can be a collective enlightened voice for our Western rivers, affirming that we must always have healthy rivers that benefit every living thing. We are, after all, made of water and pulse, of rivers and how we value rivers; our relationship to rivers is up to us.

Go to the river. Go to the river to see your image reflected back in still waters. Go to the river to feel cold current vibrating over cobble in knee-deep water. We are of the same energy, of the same waters. The Colorado River is still shaping and changing everything she touches and remains one of the great rivers of the world. But what happens when we know and love the river? As Baba Dioum, a Senegalese forestry engineer, said in 1968, "In the end, we will conserve only what we love; we will love only what we understand; and we will understand only what we are taught." What happens when we go to the river and take kids there to spark their imaginations and show them where their water comes from? Imagine how different things could be if a lot more folks knew their own water source and felt the pulse of a wild river, then shared the experience. Imagine going to the river to hear birdsong, riffles, the slap of a beaver tail; to find the thickest cottonwood; to witness the miracle of cranes; to go to the river and just breathe. Imagine the $17 billion spent annually on Colorado River recreation growing, bringing more people to the river so more of us know her, our collective voices for the river amplified and heard, saying, "Look at the river we have!" We can reimagine the possible when our relationships to water, our love of rivers, grow and develop, and our stories reflect beauty, life, and hope—when we become the river.

Recovering the endangered cottonwood-willow ecosystem wherever possible, providing all people with access to clean water, recharging groundwater for riverine health, protecting instream flows, and greening the Colorado River Delta are hopeful pieces of a holistic view for this watershed. When we become the river, these actions will be simply giving back to a watershed that all of our western lives are built upon. When we become the river, there will be no separation between us and the river, between us and crane, warbler, trout, bobcat. When we become the river, water and all of the life supported in her flow will be sacred. The Colorado River and her tributaries change everything they touch, including us. That is the river's promise.

There may just be enough water for people, wildlife, and life in flow. When we become the river.

PHOTOGRAPHER'S NOTES

OFFICIALLY, *LIVING RIVER* HAS BEEN a six-year project, going on seven so far since rafting the Yampa River with Audubon Rockies—yet it feels like thirty years in the making. When I look back on the journey, I think of all the Colorado fourteeners my wife, Marla Ofstad, and I have summited in our thirty-three years together, forty-five in total, each mountain peak the headwaters of a river, a watershed. We were hungry, deeply grounded in nature, and couldn't get enough wilderness. Together, we've chased that feeling of solitude and suffering under the weight of a heavy backpack, traversing high mountain passes between river drainages in the Elk Mountains, San Juans, and Sawatch, Gore, and Front Ranges—so many trails leading to staggering beauty and soothing our souls. And our expeditions stretched around the world to glaciers atop Kilimanjaro, in the Himalaya, the Andes, the Alps, with glaciers receding everywhere. Over time, we witnessed snowpack in the Rockies arriving late and melting off earlier, reducing flow to the Colorado River, Platte River, and Rio Grande—all of it tied to global heating and unrelenting pressure on rivers. Our zeal and curiosity for all things wilderness, for rivers pouring from mountain snowpack, only grew in intensity.

Those decades of exploring the West, from the bottom of the Grand Canyon to the highest Rocky Mountain summits, across imperiled sage and prairie, revealed life wherever rivers flow. Working across the intermountain West and with Platte Basin Timelapse, I came to realize that no place is pristine or untouched by humankind, yet functioning ecosystems can thrive with just a nudge. Nature and rivers have long memories.

Drawing on my lived experiences of an abundance of life in and along rivers, dating back to when I was a kid fishing the Rock and Mississippi Rivers with my buddy Jack Hoffman, I began sketching out a plan for the Living River story. Pragmatically, I knew covering all 1,450 miles of the main stem of the Colorado wasn't possible, or even desirable—the tributaries of the Colorado are stunning, rich in stories and biodiversity, and it's the same river, the same community anywhere in the watershed, with stories begging to be told. Why not start on the Fraser, where Marla and I had been searching for white-tailed ptarmigan high in the headwaters for years? The Fraser, after all, holds much of the Colorado River story in its thirty-two-mile length—dams and diversions before the river leaves the mountains, the big city (Denver) pulling more than half of the Fraser River through the Rockies into the watershed of the Platte. I went to see Kirk Klancke and his lovely wife, Darlene, who became fast friends and partners in telling this story.

Looking back, I had to see as many sides of the Colorado River story as I possibly could in those first two years, driving everywhere from the Wind River Range headwaters of the Green River to Arizona's borderlands. My expeditions were scrappy, and I thought of myself as a fancy dirtbag eating organic groceries from a Yeti cooler while sleeping in my truck across the West. With the simple idea of telling the story of a Living River, the idea that we must always have rivers, the first raft trip of my life on the Yampa opened a portal to the spellbinding world of living on river time. River wilderness and mountain wilderness have some of the same signatures of life unplugged: solitude and immersion in nature. Yet while rafting, the river decides the speed of travel, carrying life (and a lot of stuff) in current as rivers do. From that first raft trip, I tried to see as much of the watershed as I could, and two years in I'd covered a good bit, from the upper Green River in the southeast corner of the Greater Yellowstone region to Yuma's industrial lettuce fields in southwest Arizona. I was looking for river keepers and good stories emblematic of elsewhere in the watershed, stories that would give a sense of the grand watershed.

Working with Kirk Klancke on the Fraser, Tom Koerner at Seedskadee National Wildlife Refuge, and Martha Cooper in the Gila River headwaters, I sharpened my focus to the places featured in the chapters of this book, places I would return to over and over through the seasons, rekindling friendships while studying the nuance of a dynamic river system under unwavering pressure. Riparian habitat is wildlife habitat, and after the initial Yampa River expedition with Audubon Rockies, we floated the Grand Canyon, which became the Downstream chapter story, and Catararact Canyon from Moab to Hite Marina at the head of Lake Powell. OARS and AzRA expertly guided our raft trips, with guides educating and interpreting these great rivers beneath towering canyon walls. There is absolutely nothing like being on a wild stretch of river. I flew four aerial expeditions with LightHawk, a nonprofit organization that has been a stalwart conservation partner for more than a decade. Thank you, LightHawk, and volunteer pilots Ray Lee, Will Worthington, and Marijke Unger for generously lending this story the unique and important perspective of flight.

Pathways led to the remarkable people featured in this book, and I'm grateful to Anne Castle for patiently guiding me as I grappled with the Law of the River and the complexities of the last century that led us to this moment. Thanks to Anne and her partner Bidtah Becker, who founded the Universal Access to Clean Water for Tribal Communities project. Thank you to Alison Holloran and Abby Burk of Audubon Rockies, to Kirk Klancke on the Fraser River, to Martha Cooper on the Gila River, to Holly Richter on the San Pedro River, to Tom Koerner at Seedskadee National Wildlife Refuge, and to raft guide B. J. Boyle of Flagstaff, Arizona, for contributing mightily. Many thanks to Indigenous friends Cynthia Wilson, Elouise Wilson, Henry Wilson Sr., Jonah Yellowman, Dr. Angelo Baca, and all the kind folks I've met through our first connection at the Utah Diné Bikéyah Summer Gathering. I'm grateful for your trust and friendship. I learned the depth of Colorado River Delta restoration through Jennifer Pitt, who graciously shared a hopeful story of international collaboration and life returning to the Colorado River Delta. Thanks to Gabriela Caloca Michele, Marylu Sandoval, and Dilan Ortiz of Pronatura Noroeste for sharing the wonders of the Delta, a vision of returning the Colorado River to the sea with the Raise the River Alliance and of nature's remarkable response to restoration. Thanks to Dr. Mary Harner and Dr. Keith Geluso for so enthusiastically insisting that the Gila must be experienced. Thanks to author and educator John Fleck for your exhaustive research and writings, revealing the history and characters leading to

Marla and Dave launch a backpacking expedition in the upper Green River basin, Bridger–Teton Wilderness, Wyoming.

this moment. Thank you to Jack C. Schmidt for sharing decades of watershed knowledge via Zoom at the peak of Covid. Thanks to dear friends Michael Forsberg and Mariah Lundgren, to friends at Platte Basin Timelapse, and to my buddy Kim Lindenlaub, who grew up in the headwaters and told me "the river belongs to no one and everyone." Many more folks supported this journey, and I'm grateful.

Thank you to Helen Cherullo of Braided River for seeing the value in this story before the idea was fully formed, and to Erika Lundahl and all the wonderful people at Braided River and Mountaineers Books working to bring the story to life. Thank you, Walton Family Foundation, for generously supporting our story and leading in conservation throughout the watershed.

IN BETWEEN RIVER EXPEDITIONS, Marla and I continued our wilderness explorations. We continued our search for white-tailed ptarmigan at the headwaters of the Fraser River and held to a New Year's tradition of waking around three in the morning on New Year's Day, driving over Berthoud Pass, and snowshoeing in darkness to greet sunrise of a new year cresting the Rockies. For this project, we busted a move while backpacking in Colorado's San Juan Range, climbed Uncompahgre Peak, 14,309 feet, and camped atop Colorado's sixth-highest peak. There, we reveled in taking in the scale of the San Juan Range as sunrise painted Wetterhorn Peak's pointy summit in red.

Everything changed as Covid hit, when Marla was diagnosed with liposarcoma, the rarest of cancers. Marla approached her cancer journey with incredible resolve and stoicism, an obstacle to be overcome. She traveled through brutal chemotherapy, seeking joy, nature, and the company of dear friends in between treatments. Her optimism never cracked as her athletic body withered, and she regained strength with clean scans in the fall of 2020. With Marla back to full strength, we backpacked five times in 2021, Marla leading our way up the trail, planning the trips, making the food, gravitating to joy always. We had reached a point as a couple where we flowed like a river, our love deep and wide, where all our dreams and goals seemed possible and infinite.

But cancer returned in the fall of 2021, more surgeries followed, and Marla rallied to hike up Angels Landing (in Zion National Park) in December, where we were greeted by a family of California condors just overhead, a gift. Marla lost ground after that and fought hard every single day, always believing there was a path for her through this awful disease. There were times while writing this story when I was consciously writing just for Marla, and I would read those rough first drafts to her in the evening. She loved this story, believed in the work and in me with all her heart. We spoke often of our dreams, of wilderness, of a love so deep, of believing better days lie ahead. Our daily ritual of touching nature became a short walk and digging bare feet into warm prairie grass, giving gratitudes. Marla Jill Ofstad never, ever gave in, never lost hope, and ran out of time against cancer, passing peacefully on May 20, 2022. She was the finest person I've ever known and I never knew a love like ours was possible. Marla's passing is a seismic loss of love and light.

But Marla's undying hope against all odds is a beautiful gift. Marla would expect me to keep going to finish this story. With a heavy heart, I traveled to the Colorado River Delta and Lake Mead, then flew over the Delta with legendary pilot Will Worthington of LightHawk. There, against the backdrop of endless stories of a dying river, I witnessed young conservationists with a deep connection to the river we have, where life is returning to restoration sites with a tiny bit of water and a nudge from river keepers planting native vegetation, cottonwood, and willow. Redemption, trust, and the promise of the Colorado.

After all these thousands of miles of rivers and roads, of being swept by current and lifeblood energy, I see and feel the living Colorado River as metaphor for love, light, and hope. Today, I go to the river to heal.

May we always have rivers flowing through us.

RESOURCES

ORGANIZATIONS

Arizona Raft Adventures (AzRA), https://azraft.com
Audubon Arizona, https://az.audubon.org
Audubon Rockies, https://rockies.audubon.org
Bears Ears Inter-Tribal Coalition, www.bearsearscoalition.org
Center for Colorado River Studies, Utah State University, https://qcnr.usu.edu/coloradoriver/
Cochise Conservation and Recharge Network, https://ccrnsanpedro.org
Colorado River District, www.coloradoriverdistrict.org
Colorado River Storage Project, US Bureau of Reclamation, www.usbr.gov/uc/rm/crsp/index.html
Colorado Water Center, Colorado State University, https://watercenter.colostate.edu
East Grand [County] Water Quality Board, https://co.grand.co.us/1380/East-Grand-Water-Quality-Board
Friends of the San Pedro River, www.sanpedroriver.org
Getches-Wilkinson Center for Natural Resources, Energy, and the Environment, www.getches-wilkinsoncenter.cu.law
Grand Canyon Trust, www.grandcanyontrust.org
Grand County Learning by Doing Cooperative Effort, www.grandcountylearningbydoing.org
Grand County Water Information Network, www.gcwin.org
Headwaters River Journey, https://headwatersriverjourney.com
Indian Health Service, www.ihs.gov
International Boundary and Water Commission, www.ibwc.gov
John Fleck, www.inkstain.net
LightHawk conservation flying, www.lighthawk.org
The Nature Conservancy, www.nature.org: Arizona Water Projects, Freshwater Program, Gila River Preserve, Lichty Ecological Research Center, Ramsey Canyon Preserve, Southwest New Mexico Program
Outdoor Adventure River Specialists (OARS), www.oars.com
Platte Basin Timelapse project, https://plattebasintimelapse.com
Pronatura Noroeste, www.pronatura-noroeste.org
Raise the River Alliance, https://raisetheriver.org
Seedskadee National Wildlife Refuge, www.fws.gov/refuge/seedskadee
Sierra Club, www.sierraclub.org
Sonoran Institute, Colorado River Delta Program, https://sonoraninstitute.org/card/colorado-river-delta/
Universal Access to Clean Water for Tribal Communities project, https://tribalcleanwater.org
Trout Unlimited Headwaters Chapter, www.coheadwaters.org
Upper Colorado River Commission, www.ucrcommission.com
Upper San Pedro Partnership, https://uppersanpedropartnership.org
Utah Diné Bikéyah, www.utahdinebikeyah.org
Walton Family Foundation, www.waltonfamilyfoundation.org
WaterSMART, program of the US Bureau of Reclamation, www.usbr.gov/watersmart/
Women of Bears Ears, www.womenofbearsears.org
Wyoming Trout Unlimited, www.wyomingtu.org

PUBLICATIONS

Dioum, Baba. Paper presented at triennial meeting of General Assembly of the International Union for the Conservation of Nature and Natural Resources, New Delhi, India, 1968.

Fleck, John, and Eric Kuhn. *Science Be Dammed: How Ignoring Inconvenient Science Drained the Colorado River.* Tucson: University of Arizona Press, 2021.

Kuhn, Eric, and Lael Gilbert. "New Research Explores Hard Truths for the Future of Colorado River Management." *Colorado Water* 38, no. 1 (June 2021): 19–21. Fort Collins: Colorado Water Center, Colorado State University, 2021.

Leopold, Aldo. *A Sand County Almanac.* Oxford: Oxford University Press, 1949.

Sibley, David Allen. *Sibley Birds West: Field Guide to Birds of Western North America.* 2nd ed. New York: Knopf, 2016.

MAP SOURCES

Colorado River Watershed map source: "Colorado River Basin base map," Fig. 1 in *Colorado River Basin Water Supply and Demand Study*, US Bureau of Reclamation, 2012.

Headwaters Watershed map sources: "Mountains to Sea: The History and Future of the Colorado River," Babbit Center for Land and Water Policy, Lincoln Institute of Land Policy, and Center for Geospatial Solutions; map design by Matt Jenkins, Zachary Sugg, Chaz Baculi, Paula Randolph, and Jeff Allenby. "Colorado River BIP Grand County Region," CDSS, CDHP, CWCB, USGS, CRWCD. "City and County of Denver Board of Water Commissioners: Water Collection System," Denver Water; map by Admin Services GIS. "Colorado River above Grand Junction," US Bureau of Reclamation. "Colorado River Basin," Colorado River District, from Basin Study by US Bureau of Reclamation. "Upper Colorado River Sub Watersheds," Upper Colorado River Watershed Group; Divide Environmental and Mapping.

Bears Ears National Monument map source: US Bureau of Land Management; map by Stephanie Smith.

Gila River Watershed map sources: "National Parks within the Gila Watershed" and "The Gila Watershed," Archaeology Southwest; maps by Catherine Gilman.

San Pedro River Watershed map sources: "Mountains to Sea: The History and Future of the Colorado River," Babbit Center for Land and Water Policy, Lincoln Institute of Land Policy, and Center for Geospatial Solutions; map design by Matt Jenkins, Zachary Sugg, Chaz Baculi, Paula Randolph, and Jeff Allenby. "San Pedro River Surface Water Extent June 2020," The Nature Conservancy.

The Colorado River Delta Region map sources: "Downstream from the Morelos Dam, the Colorado River Delta," Yale School of the Environment; map by David Lindroth. "Mountains to Sea: The History and Future of the Colorado River," Babbit Center for Land and Water Policy, Lincoln Institute of Land Policy, and Center for Geospatial Solutions; map design by Matt Jenkins, Zachary Sugg, Chaz Baculi, Paula Randolph, and Jeff Allenby. "Colorado River Delta Restoration Sites," Sonoran Institute.

ABOUT THE AUTHOR

Conservation photographer and author **DAVE SHOWALTER** is focused on the American West. Dave works throughout the ecosystems of the intermountain West and has published two books prior to *Living River*: *Sage Spirit—The American West at a Crossroads*, also with Braided River, and *Prairie Thunder—The Nature of Colorado's Great Plains*, with Skyline Press. Dave is a Senior Fellow in the International League of Conservation Photographers and a longtime contributor and partner of Platte Basin Timelapse. Dave works in partnership with numerous conservation groups, including Audubon Rockies, The Nature Conservancy, and the Trout Unlimited Headwaters Chapter, on the Living River project. With *Living River* and conservation storytelling, Dave seeks to take readers on a journey to see ourselves as part of nature and the community of living things, engendering empathy, caring, and love of the natural world—the genesis of meaningful conservation. Dave is based in Arvada, Colorado.

Dave Showalter journals at a pinch point along the Gunnison River on a solo backpack in the depths of Black Canyon of the Gunnison National Park, Colorado.

In gratitude to the Walton Family Foundation for their generous support that made this book possible

WALTON FAMILY
FOUNDATION

ABOUT THE WALTON FAMILY FOUNDATION

The Walton Family Foundation is, at its core, a family-led foundation. Three generations of the descendants of our founders, Sam and Helen Walton, and their spouses work together to lead the foundation and create access to opportunity for people and communities. We work in three areas: improving K–12 education, protecting rivers and oceans and the communities they support, and investing in our home region of Northwest Arkansas and the Arkansas-Mississippi Delta. To learn more, visit waltonfamilyfoundation.org and follow us on Facebook, Twitter, and Instagram.

BRAIDED RIVER

BRAIDED RIVER, the conservation imprint of Mountaineers Books, combines photography and writing to bring a fresh perspective to key environmental issues facing western North America's wildest places. Our books reach beyond the printed page as we take these distinctive voices and vision to a wider audience through lectures, exhibits, and multimedia events. Our goal is to build public support for wilderness preservation campaigns and inspire public action. This work is made possible through the book sales and contributions made to Braided River, a 501(c)(3) nonprofit organization. Please visit BraidedRiver.org for more information on events, exhibits, speakers, and how to contribute to this work.

Braided River books may be purchased for corporate, educational, or other promotional sales. For special discounts and information, contact our sales department at 800.553.4453 or mbooks@mountaineersbooks.org.

THE MOUNTAINEERS, founded in 1906, is a nonprofit outdoor activity and conservation organization, whose mission is "to explore, study, preserve, and enjoy the natural beauty of the outdoors. . . . " Mountaineers Books supports this mission by publishing travel and natural history guides, instructional texts, and works on conservation and history.

See our website to explore our catalog of 700 outdoor titles:
Mountaineers Books
1001 SW Klickitat Way, Suite 201
Seattle, WA 98134
800.553.4453
www.mountaineersbooks.org

Printed in China. Manufactured in Canada on FSC®-certified paper, using soy-based ink.

For more information and updates, please visit www.LivingRiverColorado.org.

Braided River Executive Director: Helen Cherullo
Braided River Deputy Director: Erika Lundahl
Managing Editor: Janet Kimball
Developmental Editor: Linda Gunnarson
Copyeditor and Project Editor: Kris Fulsaas
Cover and Book Designer: Amelia von Wolffersdorff
Cartographer: Martha Bostwick

Front cover photo: *The Nankoweap granaries stand high above the Colorado River at river mile 53 in the Grand Canyon inner gorge where Ancestral Puebloan people stored pumpkin seeds and corn irrigated in the Colorado River floodplain. Humans have occupied Grand Canyon environs since the Clovis Culture, around 9200* BC. Page 1: *Over two million years, the Gunnison River has carved the deep gorge barely penetrated by sunlight in Black Canyon of the Gunnison National Park, Colorado. The Gunnison, a major tributary of the Colorado, is just forty feet wide at its narrowest point, its many voices echoing between the walls of stone.* Pages 2–3: *Morning light pierces an opening in Canyonlands National Park, Utah, to paint rock formations of the Doll House and the Colorado River in reflected gold during a raft trip through Cataract Canyon with Audubon Rockies.* Pages 4–5: *The dizzying view from the north rim of Black Canyon of the Gunnison National Park overlooks a remarkable 1,700 feet of vertical. The Gunnison River and time continue shaping everything in view, creating a spectacular chasm in the sagelands. The Gunnison's confluence with the Colorado River is in the city of Grand Junction, Colorado.* Page 6: *The Yampa River winds under towering cliff faces on its journey west to meet the Green River in Dinosaur National Monument, Utah.* (*LightHawk aerial support*) Last page: *Coated in pollen, a* Bombus bifarius *bumblebee lifts off from golden autumn rabbitbrush on the north rim of Black Canyon of the Gunnison National Park, Colorado. Declining globally, wild bees play an important role as pollinators of native flora and crops.* Back cover photo: *Signatures of a wild river are written in deep blues of evening in the Gila Box of the upper Gila River, Arizona. A major tributary of the Colorado, the Gila flows over cobble, with autumn golds and oranges of cottonwood and sycamore indicating a healthy undammed stream with a natural flood regime. Deeper study reveals unparalleled wildlife richness.*

Library of Congress Control Number: 2022948621

ISBN 978-1-68051-632-6

An independent nonprofit publisher since 1960